THE
LES MIMOSAS
COOKBOOK

THE
LES MIMOSAS
COOKBOOK

SARAH & DENIS LA TOUCHE

FOR FOOD LOVERS . . . EVERYWHERE

ACKNOWLEDGEMENTS

Our warmest thanks go to Annie and Graham, for their friendship, the inspiration to write this book, and for selling the idea to the publisher; Marie, Hélène and André, for their generosity and friendship, for opening their house and table to us, and for sharing their recipes; our fellow *Roquebrunaises* and *Roquebrunais* for making us welcome in their village, and allowing us to be a part of their lives.

BY THE SAME AUTHORS

Kiwi Kwickie Kookbook
Europe on a plate

TO CONTACT LES MIMOSAS

Avenue des Orangers
34460 Roquebrun
FRANCE
Telephone & Fax 04 67 89 61 36
e-mail: la-touche.les-mimosas@wanadoo.fr
http://perso.wanadoo.fr/les-mimosas

Published by Godwit Publishing Limited
15 Rawene Road, P.O. Box 34-683
Birkenhead, Auckland, New Zealand

First published 1997

ISBN 1 86962 017 8

Cover design by Mirella Monteiro
Printed in Singapore

CONTENTS

INTRODUCTION

In 1992 we decided to follow our dream and moved to the south of France. We bought a charming nineteenth-century *maison de maître* in a very pretty village in the Languedoc region and restored it to create an elegant country guest-house serving good, honest cuisine and good regional wines.

More than anything it was our love of French food and wine and the French way of life that inspired us. The simple rhythm of life in a small wine-growing village and a fervent appreciation of the French passion for food and their innate ability to marry flavours with good wine created plenty of incentive for us to up stakes, transfer hemispheres and swap one culture for another. Our learning curve rapidly developed into a vertical step-ladder and we worked harder than we ever imagined.

In France, food and wine are lifetime occupations — there is no such thing as a bad moment to learn about a new wine or discover a new taste sensation. And all the better if it can be done in the company of those who appreciate the finer things in life. After five short, action-packed years, we have discovered more about French food and wine than we thought possible and yet we have only scratched the surface.

The idea for this cookbook was born while enjoying one of those pastimes we favour most in life, lunching with good friends on our terrace in the shade of the grape arbour, one deliciously warm September afternoon. Our friends had just suggested that the time

had come for us to record, in the form of a cookbook, all those recipes we had been cooking for our guests over the years. A bit of digesting was required, but not too much, before we decided that they had a point. After all, it did occupy the better part of our lives. And so our 'French Collection' was born.

We had been discussing one of our favourite topics,

SARAH AT THE FRONT DOOR OF LES MIMOSAS
RETURNING FROM THE BOULANGERIE WITH THE BREAD
FOR BREAKFAST

the advantages and disadvantages of eating seasonal produce — how produce grown naturally, in its own season and time and ripened with real sunshine, tastes so much better than something that is raised in artificial surroundings, is sprayed to keep it fresh and stuck on a supermarket shelf under specialised lighting to make it all look good.

Happily, seasonal cooking is still very much a part of French cuisine, but as the world marches on under the name of progress we are becoming trapped in a world of convenience where we are consuming more and more processed and pre-packaged foods, artificially ripened fruit and vegetables, and where obesity, heart disease and cancer are very real modern-day health concerns. Even in France, the land of gastronomy, convenience foods are posing a threat to the art of French cuisine.

Since moving to our village we have become avid supporters of the much-publicised 'Mediterranean diet', but even more importantly, the use of fresh produce eaten seasonally. And that is the backbone of this book — quality, good-tasting, seasonal produce, cooked simply. It almost sounds too easy. But as many of the world's great chefs purport, if you start with good produce, how can you go wrong!

So, with spring's arrival we gorge on fresh artichokes and asparagus, new green beans, peas in their pods and earthy potatoes. The new sheep and goat cheeses begin to appear. Deliciously perfumed strawberries are followed by the cherry season, one of our favourite times of the year. Then comes summer, with tomatoes and aubergines ripened in the sun and picked at just the right time, and a host of irresistible stone fruits.

In the autumn wild mushrooms abound, chestnuts and walnuts are gathered, the beginning of the citrus and pear season arrives. The olives are harvested and cured or pressed for oil. Root vegetables begin to appear, summer garlic is hung to store over the colder months and a wide range of pulses are dried to use as a base in soups and stews to satisfy hungry winter appetites. There are always salad greens available — the sweeter tender varieties in spring and summer, the hardy more bitter breeds during the colder months. Each fruit and vegetable finds its rightful place in the annual food table. We have never been healthier and there is never a question of boredom with what we have to eat.

One of the popular misconceptions about French food is that it is more often than not overly rich, with lots of heavy sauces. This may be the case with *haute cuisine*, which in real terms only accounts for a highly publicised, small percentage of restaurants in France. But when it comes to country *cuisine familiale*, the style of cooking becomes much simpler with plenty of robust flavours, lots of herbs and vegetables. The meat will often be served with the juices it was cooked in instead of a weighty sauce.

Many French still take their main meal at midday, which makes perfect sense for a healthy digestive system. The evening meal will then be something light like a soup or gratin of vegetables, with perhaps some cold cuts of meat. And a glass of red wine is obligatory, though usually just a glass rather than an entire bottle. All in all, balance prevails and *la grande bouffe* is reserved for special family occasions and Sunday lunch outings.

Many of the recipes in this book are adaptations of French family cuisine that we serve on a daily basis at Les Mimosas. It is by no means a definitive collection but it is the sort of food you would be served if you visited a French family in the heart of the southern countryside. A number of the recipes have been passed down through several generations of matriarchs and we have been fortunate enough to enjoy them, and their creators' generosity in sharing their recipes with us.

Some of the recipes have no origins in France but are old favourites that we have served to our guests over time and which have found a popular place in our repertoire. As we must cater for all tastes, we hope there is something for everyone.

The book was written in France with non-French cooks in mind. There are no complex sauces or reductions and the main fats used are quality olive oils, duck fat — which is surprisingly good for you if used in moderation — and unsalted butter for pastry and desserts. Some of the ingredients are typically French and may be difficult to find outside the French marketplace. However, substitutes can always be found and although they will alter the final outcome of the dish, the results will still be satisfying and tasty. We have noted substitute ingredients where possible but do not be afraid to take up the challenge and search out new ingredients for yourself. Improvisation is the middle name of every great cook! For example, a good Toulouse sausage (pure pork with no breadcrumbs in sight) will most likely be very hard to come by. But why not try a good venison sausage instead, or a pork sausage from the Asian wholesaler. Some people will have trusty butchers who can advise and supply the ingredients to

make your own pure pork sausage if you are really passionate about it, or they might admire your perspicacity and even make a pork sausage just for you. Many treasures can be found with an active imagination and a bit of good detective work. Your kitchen supply cupboard, repertoire and guests will benefit enormously in the long run.

Above all, these are dishes that we love to cook and serve to our guests, and this book is an expression of the pleasure we continue to find in doing that. We do not imagine we will ever trade in our blue aprons, the mark of an apprentice chef, for white ones — there is still so much to discover and it is still so much fun.

Sarah and Denis La Touche
Roquebrun, France
May 1997

SPRING

BAKED EGGS

OEUFS EN COCOTTE

Prepared in individual ramekins, this dish is delightfully different, and can be adapted for eating all year round by changing the herb mixed with the crème fraîche. It is particularly good with steamed sorrel or spinach as well.

SERVES 4

4 EGGS
A GOOD BUNCH TARRAGON, CHOPPED, OR A BUNCH OF
SPINACH OR SORREL, STEAMED
4 TABLESPOONS CRÈME FRAÎCHE
SALT AND PEPPER

Take 4 small ramekins about 7 cm (3 inches) wide, and butter the insides.

Mix the chopped tarragon or steamed sorrel or spinach with the crème fraîche, season, and spoon a tablespoon of the mixture into each ramekin.

Break an egg over the top of each, and season the raw egg. Place the ramekins in a baking dish, and pour hot water around them until it reaches halfway up the sides of the ramekins.

Bake in a hot oven, 220°C (425°F; gas mark 7), for 8–12 minutes, until the egg is just done but still wobbly on top.

Serve immediately.

SALT COD PÂTÉ

BRANDADE DE MORUE

This is a Languedoc speciality made from salt cod, olive oil and milk, which may not sound very appetising in words, but once you try the real thing you will see why it is difficult to resist. The name is derived from the old Occitan verb *brander*, which means to stir, and the numerous variations on the recipe depend on whether you live to the east or west of the mouth of the river Rhône. In Provence, recipes will include garlic but traditionally Languedocien recipes are made without it; some add white bread. In the recipe that follows we have included the garlic as an option, so you can experiment for yourself; if you are really addicted to the taste of garlic and cannot live without it, the toasted bread that accompanies the brandade can always be rubbed with a freshly peeled clove to give it that extra zing.

SERVES 6

225 g (8 oz) SALT COD — IF YOU CANNOT GET HOLD OF
SALT COD TRY ANY FIRM, YET FLAKY FISH LIKE
HADDOCK OR MULLET
6 TABLESPOONS OLIVE OIL
2 LARGE CLOVES GARLIC, PEELED AND CRUSHED
100 ml (3 fl oz) WARM MILK
PEPPER
JUICE OF A LEMON
LIGHTLY TOASTED BREAD
CHOPPED PARSLEY TO GARNISH

To desalt the cod, cut it into pieces and place in a colander. Put the colander in a basin of cold water for 24 hours, changing the water every 3–4 hours. It is important that the cod is well washed of salt.

Rinse and drain, and place in a saucepan. Cover with cold water and slowly bring to the boil. Cover and simmer for 8 minutes. When the fish is cooked, drain it and remove any skin and bones, and break into flaky pieces.

In another saucepan, heat 2 tablespoons of olive oil, add the fish and stir over a low heat. Add the garlic, if you wish, then slowly add the rest of the olive oil. The mixture should resemble a thickish paste. Slowly begin to add the warmed milk, little by little, stirring all the while, until the mixture resembles a purée. Add the pepper and lemon juice, to taste.

Serve warm or cold with a sprinkling of chopped parsley and slices of toasted rye bread or baguette.

BRANDADE OF SMOKED HADDOCK

BRANDADE DE HADDOCK FUMÉ

SERVES 6

2 PAIRS HOT-SMOKED HADDOCK FILLETS
450 ml (14 fl oz) WATER AND MILK, MIXED HALF AND HALF
1 SPRIG OF FRESH THYME
1 BAY LEAF
8 PEPPERCORNS
450 g (1 lb) FLOURY POTATOES, PEELED
150 ml (5 fl oz) EXTRA VIRGIN OLIVE OIL
3 LARGE CLOVES GARLIC, PEELED AND CRUSHED
2 TABLESPOONS CAPERS, CHOPPED ROUGHLY
3 TABLESPOONS EACH CHOPPED, FRESH PARSLEY AND
CHIVES OR CRESS

Place the fish fillets in a wide pan with the milk and water, thyme, bay leaf and peppercorns. Bring to the boil for a few minutes then allow to cool in the liquid.

At the same time, boil the potatoes until cooked, then mash. Cover to keep warm.

Strain the liquid from the smoked haddock, and put to one side. Skin and bone the haddock, flaking the fish as you go. Heat the olive oil in a large saucepan and stir in a spoonful of fish. Add more of the fish spoonful by spoonful, over a medium heat, and continue beating. Stir in the garlic, capers and herbs, then beat in the mashed potato. By now the mixture should have absorbed all the olive oil and be light in consistency. Add some of the reserved cooking juices to adjust if necessary.

Season with freshly ground pepper and drizzle with olive oil. Serve as a pâté with bread or toast, or as an entrée, with a freshly dressed green salad to one side.

MUSSELS WITH FRESH HERBS

MOULES AU VERT

An inspired change from the traditional moules marinières, this recipe uses a superb mixture of fresh herbs to create a delicate and memorable entrée. Use small, sweet mussels for this dish, and if you cannot get hold of sorrel use a little lemon juice in its place.

SERVES 4

2 kg (4 lb 6 oz) SMALL, TENDER MUSSELS
50 g (2 oz) UNSALTED BUTTER
2 SWEET ONIONS, COARSELY CHOPPED
4 SPRIGS FLAT-LEAFED PARSLEY
2 STALKS YOUNG CELERY
1 TEASPOON COARSE-GRAINED SEA SALT
1 TEASPOON FRESHLY GROUND BLACK PEPPER
125 g (4 oz) CHERVIL, COARSELY CHOPPED
450 g (1 lb) SORREL, COARSELY CHOPPED
125 g (4 oz) FLAT-LEAFED PARSLEY, CHOPPED
2 TABLESPOONS CHOPPED TARRAGON
125 ml (4 fl oz) DRY WHITE WINE
125 ml (4 fl oz) FISH STOCK
100 ml (3 fl oz) CREAM

Scrub the mussels in lots of cold water, discarding any that are broken or slightly open.

Put them in a deep stockpot with half the butter, the onion, parsley sprigs, celery, salt and pepper. Cover and cook on a high heat for about 10 minutes, shaking the pot vigorously from time to time, until the shells have opened. Discard any mussels that remain closed. Tip the mussels into a colander and reserve the cooking liquid.

In a frying pan, melt the rest of the butter and add the chervil, sorrel, chopped parsley and tarragon. Add the cooking liquid from the mussels and the white wine. Add the stock and cream, and stir until the sauce is smooth.

Return the mussels to the stockpot, pour over the sauce and reheat. Turn out into a large warmed serving dish, with the sauce poured over the mussels.

RADISH LEAF SOUP

SOUPE DE FANES DE RADIS

The French are marvels at making use of every portion of fruit, vegetables and meat. Nothing is wasted in a good French kitchen. This soup rather resembles watercress soup, with a clean, delicate flavour and a twang of sharpness, thanks to the radishes. What better way to use the green part of the radish! In a French household the soup might be followed by a bowl of the radishes that belonged to the tops, served simply on their own with some butter and a few grains of sea salt.

SERVES 4

A FEW KNOBS OF BUTTER
1 ONION, DICED
THE LEAVES OF 3 BUNCHES OF RADISHES, WASHED,
DRAINED AND CHOPPED ROUGHLY
3 POTATOES, PEELED AND CUT INTO PIECES
1 LITRE (2 PINTS) CHICKEN STOCK OR 2 CHICKEN STOCK
CUBES DISSOLVED IN 1 LITRE (2 PINTS) HOT WATER
SALT AND PEPPER
FRESHLY GRATED NUTMEG
6 RADISHES, GRATED
125 g (4 oz) CRÈME FRAÎCHE, BEATEN TO THICKEN
4 SLICES WHOLEMEAL BAGUETTE
A FEW BRANCHES CHERVIL, CHOPPED

In a saucepan, melt a few knobs of butter and sweat the onion gently. Add the chopped radish leaves, potatoes, chicken stock, freshly ground pepper and a small amount of grated nutmeg. Let this cook uncovered for about 40 minutes over a medium heat. The liquid will reduce by about a quarter. Check the seasonings and add salt if necessary.

In the meantime, add the grated radish to the beaten crème fraîche and place in a side dish. Brown the rounds of baguette under the grill and put in a bread basket.

When the soup is cooked, pass it through a sieve or blend until smooth in a food processor. Reheat and turn out into a warmed tureen. Sprinkle with chopped chervil and serve with the radish cream on the croûtons.

ASPARAGUS WITH VINAIGRETTE

ASPERGES À LA VINAIGRETTE

Asparagus has been a great delicacy in France since the time of Louis XIV, who had a great fondness for this diuretic vegetable. There are three or four varieties grown commercially here, and there is also a wild variety which

To remove the stringy part of the asparagus stalk, take it in both hands and bend the stalk gently. It will snap at the point where the soft edible part ends. Treat each stalk this way, trim any untidy ends and rinse under cold water.

Stand the asparagus upright in a proper asparagus steamer with the water level low enough to keep the tips uncovered, and steam gently for approximately 10 minutes. If you do not have a steamer, a deep wide pan will suffice. Put the asparagus into boiling salted water, lying down in this case, for about 5 minutes. As soon as the asparagus is tender, drain it and run cold water over it immediately, and leave to cool in a colander.

Cut 4 strips of green leek leaves, about 2.5 cm (1 inch) wide, and blanch them in boiling water until soft and pliable, then drain.

Make up the vinaigrette and leave to meld.

TO SERVE: On 4 separate dinner plates, arrange the asparagus into 4 'bouquets'. Tie around the base of each with the blanched leek leaves, and fan out the tips a little. Drizzle over the vinaigrette, and grind over some fresh black pepper and coarse-grained sea salt. Serve with chunks of freshly baked rye bread to mop up the juices.

NOTE: The asparagus can be replaced with artichokes, preferably the large, plump purple variety. Allow 1 artichoke per person. To cook, place the artichokes in a large saucepan, cover with cold, salted water, and add a dash of vinegar. Weigh the artichokes down by putting a plate on top of them. Cover with a lid and bring to the boil. Simmer steadily for 15–20 minutes, depending on their size, until they are tender. Transfer to a colander and leave to cool.

TO SERVE: Trim any stray leaves from the base of the stalks. Cut in half with a very sharp knife and remove the furry 'choke' between the base of the leaves and the heart. Place them with the interiors facing upwards on a large plate, spoon over the dressing, and garnish with lots of ground pepper.

is much thinner and slightly more bitter, but nonetheless delicious prepared in a light omelette or Blanquette de Veau (see page 74). We are fortunate enough to live in an area where both green and wild asparagus grow. During the months of February and March it is possible to gather wild asparagus in the countryside, a pleasant pastime to wile away a Sunday afternoon after a hearty lunch. And from early March onwards the local producers spoil us with beautiful fine bunches of the fresh green commercially grown variety, which we like best with a good tangy balsamic vinaigrette. For an entrée, allow 300 g (10 oz) of asparagus per person.

SERVES 4

1.25 kg (2 lb 12 oz) FRESH GREEN OR PURPLE ASPARAGUS
4 STRIPS OF GREEN LEEK LEAVES

VINAIGRETTE

50 ml (2 fl oz) OLIVE OIL
25 ml (1 fl oz) BALSAMIC VINEGAR
1 CLOVE GARLIC, PEELED AND
FLATTENED UNDER THE BLADE OF A KNIFE
PINCH OF SUGAR
SALT AND PEPPER

BEAN FRY

HARICOTS VERTS AUX CREVETTES

This recipe is usually made with scarlet runner beans, but here we use French green beans, which are delicious, although not quite the same taste.

SERVES 4

50 g (2 oz) DRIED PRAWNS
2 TABLESPOONS VEGETABLE OIL
1 ONION, SLICED
450 g (1 lb) GREEN BEANS, TOPPED AND TAILED, SLICED
GROUND BLACK PEPPER AND SALT, TO TASTE
1–2 TEASPOONS WORCESTERSHIRE SAUCE

Soak the prawns in 500 ml of water overnight. Drain before use.

Heat the oil in a pan to a medium heat, add the onion and sauté until it starts to brown. Add the beans, prawns, seasoning and Worcestershire sauce. Cover and cook for 4–5 minutes on a high heat, stirring and shaking the pan to avoid burning. Serve and eat hot.

GREEN BEAN SALAD

SALADE DE HARICOTS VERTS

We are self-confessed green bean freaks in this household, not least in the spring, when the new green beans start appearing on the producers' stalls in our local markets. I appear, at least twice a week, in front of our favourite stall-holder with a large basket at the ready.

SERVES 4–6

1 MEDIUM RED PEPPER, ROASTED, PEELED AND SLICED FINELY (SEE PAGE 65)
500 g (1 lb 2 oz) FRENCH GREEN BEANS, TOPPED AND TAILED
100 g (4 oz) PINE NUTS
200 g (7 oz) LARDONS OR STREAKY BACON, CHOPPED
2–3 LEEKS, TRIMMED AND SLICED INTO JULIENNES

FOR THE VINAIGRETTE

50 ml (2 fl oz) FIRST-PRESSING OLIVE OIL
25 ml (1 fl oz) BALSAMIC VINEGAR
PINCH OF BROWN SUGAR
1 CLOVE GARLIC, FLATTENED UNDER THE BLADE OF A KNIFE
COARSELY GROUND BLACK PEPPER AND SEA SALT

Prepare the pepper in advance (we keep a jar of them in our refrigerator).

Wash the green beans in a colander and drain. Cook the beans very lightly in a steamer, so that they retain their crunchiness — about 5–8 minutes, no longer. Rinse immediately in lots of cold water, so the beans cool rapidly and keep their vivid colour. Drain and put to one side.

In a dry heavy-bottomed frying pan, roast the pine nuts. They contain their own oil and do not need any lubrication. When nicely brown, put to one side to cool.

In the same pan, sauté the lardons in their own fat until golden. Remove from the pan with a slotted spoon and drain on a paper towel.

Take the julienned leeks and sauté in the bacon fat until tender. Remove and drain.

Make up the vinaigrette in plenty of time so that the garlic has time to infuse with the oil and vinegar.

To make up the salad, place all the ingredients in a large bowl and pour over the vinaigrette. Toss thoroughly so that all the vegetables are coated in the sauce. Arrange on individual plates in a little mountain, and garnish with freshly ground pepper and sea salt.

GOAT CHEESE TARTLETS

TARTELETTES AU FROMAGE DE CHÈVRE

A spring or summertime treat for a delicious entrée or light lunch. The flavours are refreshing and very much the essence of the Midi. If you have the time, this recipe can be adapted to tiny tartlet moulds and served as an hors d'oeuvre.

SERVES 6

250 g (9 oz) PÂTE BRISÉE (SEE PAGE 121)

FILLING

1 TABLESPOON OLIVE OIL
1 MEDIUM-SIZED SWEET ONION, CHOPPED FINELY
1 LARGE CLOVE GARLIC, CRUSHED OR FINELY CHOPPED
450 g (1 lb) TOMATOES, PEELED, SEEDED AND CHOPPED
1/2 TEASPOON CASTOR SUGAR
SEVERAL SPRIGS FRESH THYME
6 ANCHOVY FILLETS, CHOPPED
SALT AND PEPPER, FRESHLY GROUND
250 g (9 oz) GOAT CHEESE, CRUMBLED

Prepare the pâte brisée in advance and chill for 30 minutes.

Heat the oven to 200°C (400°F; gas mark 6).

In a heavy-bottomed frying pan, heat the olive oil and sauté the onion and garlic until soft, about 5 minutes. Add the tomatoes, sugar, thyme, anchovies, salt and pepper, and keeping the mixture uncovered cook for about 30 minutes, until almost all the liquid has evaporated and the mixture is mushy, almost a lumpy purée.

Roll out the pastry and line 6 lightly buttered 10-cm (4-inch) tartlet tins. Prick the pastry and loosely cover with a piece of tinfoil. Into the tinfoil, pour some white haricot beans to weigh the pastry down. This is to stop the pastry case rising when you bake it blind. Bake in the oven for 10–12 minutes, until the pastry is slightly cooked. Place the haricot beans in a jar for next time; discard the foil.

Crumble the goat cheese into the tomato and herb mixture and combine.

Spoon the filling into the partially cooked pastry cases and put back in the oven for another 10 minutes until cooked so that the goat cheese has melted into the tomato mixture.

The tartlets can be served hot, warm or cold, with some fresh thyme sprinkled over them and a robustly dressed salad as an accompaniment.

ROQUEFORT TIMBALES WITH SPRING SALAD

TIMBALES DE ROQUEFORT ET SALADE DE PRINTEMPS

Along with spring in France comes a whole variety of new season's sheep and goat cheeses. And along with the new cheeses come a host of tasty salad greens. A marriage of these new-season products can represent something close to heaven on a plate — all the expectancy and youth of a new season, bounding forth to take your tastebuds hostage. These timbales are made with Roquefort sheep cheese, which is made in a village of the same name, not far from us. But you can equally well substitute a good goat cheese or a blue cheese with a crumbly texture for the Roquefort.

SERVES 6

450 g (1 lb) ROQUEFORT CHEESE
4 EGGS
500 g (1 lb 2 oz) SALAD GREENS, SUCH AS ROQUETTE, MÂCHE OR LAMB'S LETTUCE, CHERVIL, OAK LEAF LETTUCE, PURSLANE, DANDELION
1/2 CUP VINAIGRETTE (SEE PAGE 120)
A HANDFUL OF BLACK OLIVES AND THYME FLOWERS FOR GARNISH

Preheat the oven to 180°C (350°F; gas mark 4).

In a food processor or with a mixing wand, combine the Roquefort cheese and eggs until smooth.

Butter 6 small ramekins and divide the mixture among them. Place the ramekins in a shallow pan and pour in enough hot water so that it comes halfway up the sides. Bake for 20–25 minutes, or until the tops are puffed and golden. Remove the ramekins from the water bath and allow to cool until the timbales are tepid.

In a large bowl, toss the salad greens with the vinaigrette. Invert the timbales on to individual serving plates and surround each with salad. Garnish each timbale with some thyme flowers, and the salad with black olives.

DEEP-FRIED LITTLE FISHES

FRITURE

In our local market we can buy fish called *Jols* at the fish stall, which are an example of *de la friture*. These are little fishes, which are only 5 cm (2 inches) when fully grown, and which are used to make this delicious dish. It is best to use a deep-fryer if you have one. If not, a frying pan with 2 cm (1 inch) of oil will do.

SERVES 4

225 g (8 oz) LITTLE FISHES
2–3 TABLESPOONS FLOUR
PEPPER AND SALT
OLIVE OIL
1 LEMON, SLICED

In a bowl, mix the flour, pepper and salt. Add the little fishes and coat lightly with the flour mixture.

Heat the olive oil in a deep-fryer or frying pan to a high heat. When it is just starting to give off a blueish haze throw in the dusted little fishes, and cook for a few minutes until the exteriors are crisp and starting to brown. Do not stir as you will break up the little fishes.

Serve immediately, with lemon squeezed over. Consume with gusto, with a well-chilled dry white or rosé wine.

TROUT WITH FENNEL

TRUITE AU FENOUIL

SERVES 6

1 FRESH TROUT, 1.5–3 kg (3–7 lb), CLEANED AND GUTTED
OR
6 SMALL TROUT, CLEANED AND GUTTED
SEVERAL KNOBS OF BUTTER
A BUNCH OF FENNEL FRONDS, WELL WASHED (THE
COMMON FENNEL WEED WILL DO OR TRY SORREL)
1–2 TOMATOES, SLICED
1 MILD ONION, FINELY SLICED, OR A SMALL BUNCH OF
SPRING ONIONS, CHOPPED
1–2 LEMONS, FINELY SLICED
250–375 ml (8–12 fl oz) FRUITY WHITE OR ROSÉ WINE
(IF USING A FISH KETTLE, ADD 250 ml (8 fl oz) OF FISH
STOCK TO THE WINE)
3–4 TABLESPOONS GOOD TANGY OLIVE OIL
GROUND BLACK PEPPER AND SALT

There is a trout farm at the top of our valley, where we regularly purchase plump, fresh rainbow trout of around 2–3 kg apiece. On our way home we often make time for an agreeable stop to embrace the views — a glorious valley of vines, cherry and almond orchards and sweeping river bends. In summer, we collect a few sprigs of wild fennel which will be added when the fish is cooked.

Ideally, trout should be cooked in a fish kettle so that it does not dry out. For those who do not possess such elaborate equipment, a good old-fashioned roasting pan will do, with a cake grill placed in the bottom of it for the fish to sit on. If you cannot get hold of fresh trout, try sea bass, snapper or farmed salmon. They will adapt well to this recipe, just make sure whatever fish you use is FRESH.

A word about the freshness of trout. If you have been given a trout and want to be sure it is fresh, feel the skin of the fish. It should be translucent, supple and *slimy*. The sliminess is a sure sign of the freshness, the result of a natural process where the fish emits a mucus to protect itself.

This recipe is an ideal way to capture and enhance all the natural flavours of this great freshwater fish.

Place the fish on cooking foil laid over the grill in a deepish baking tray. Butter the nose, fins and tail of the trout so that they do not stick to the foil during cooking. Into the stomach cavity place the fennel sprigs, sliced tomatoes and onion. Place the lemon slices along the side of the fish and pour over the wine. Drizzle the olive oil over the fish and season with freshly ground pepper and salt. Loosely wrap the foil over the fish and close securely. Make sure there is some liquid in the bottom of the cooking tray — a little water or fish stock will do — and place the tray in a moderate oven, 180°C (350°F; gas mark 4). If you are using a fish kettle, you will not need to bother with the cooking foil, but add some fish stock to the wine. Cooking time, between 20 and 50 minutes, will vary according to the size and quantity of fish, but basically it is far better to undercook than overcook trout. To test if the trout is cooked, gently pull at the back fin of the fish. If it comes away easily, the fish will be cooked.

Serve with boiled new potatoes and a fresh salad.

POACHED CHICKEN BREASTS WITH TARRAGON

BLANCS DE POULET POCHÉS À L'ESTRAGON

A light and tasty dish with all the concentrated flavours of a warm spring evening. Best served with a light dry rosé or white wine, a large bowl of steamed, buttery beans and new potatoes.

SERVES 4

4 CHICKEN BREASTS
SALT AND PEPPER, FRESHLY GROUND
2-3 TABLESPOONS OLIVE OIL IN WHICH THE TOMATOES
(SEE BELOW) HAVE BEEN PRESERVED
2 SHALLOTS, FINELY CHOPPED
200 g (7 oz) SUN-DRIED TOMATOES, CHOPPED
250 ml (8 fl oz) MUSCAT
3 TABLESPOONS CONCENTRATED CHICKEN STOCK
LARGE BUNCH TARRAGON

Season the chicken breasts with freshly ground sea salt and pepper.

Take a deep frying pan with a heavy base, and heat the oil. On a low heat, brown the chicken breasts on both sides. Remove from the pan with a slotted spoon, and put to one side.

Sauté the shallots on a medium heat, and when slightly brown add the sun-dried tomatoes. Raise the heat and pour in the muscat and stock. Poach the tomatoes for about 5 minutes. When they begin to soften, and the cooking juices have reduced a little, return the chicken to the pan and add the tarragon. Lower the heat and poach the chicken at a steady simmer, uncovered, for 10–15 minutes until the meat is tender and very slightly pink inside. Arrange the chicken breasts on a serving dish and keep warm.

Raise the heat again and if need be reduce the poaching liquids a little more. The sauce will not thicken but the flavours will intensify. Spoon the reduction over the chicken and decorate with fresh sprigs of tarragon.

BABY SPRING CHICKEN WITH TARRAGON

POUSSIN PRINTANIER

If you are fortunate enough to have a small herb garden, be it in pots on the kitchen sill or in a sunny corner of the garden, one of the most exciting times of the year is when the perennial herbs start to come away again with young, tender spring shoots. Of all the wonderful herbs to be grown, nothing seems to signify spring more than tarragon. Its fine, delicate flavour is perfect for seasoning chicken, and flavouring oils and vinegars. It likes a well-drained, sunny aspect and seems to prefer a drier climate to a humid one. Tarragon is ideal for drying in bunches, which can be hung upside down in a cool, dry place, and like basil and parsley it can be frozen too.

SERVES 4

4 POUSSINS (BABY SPRING CHICKENS)
SALT AND PEPPER TO SEASON
2 TABLESPOONS LIGHT OLIVE OIL
2 MEDIUM LEEKS, CHOPPED FINELY
4 MEDIUM TOMATOES, SKINNED, SEEDED AND CHOPPED
100 g (3 oz) PINE NUTS, LIGHTLY ROASTED IN A DRY PAN
2 TABLESPOONS FRESH, COARSELY CHOPPED TARRAGON
150 ml (5 fl oz) MUSCAT OR WHITE WINE
100 ml (3 fl oz) CREAM
SEVERAL SPRIGS FRESH TARRAGON TO GARNISH

Season the poussins with freshly ground sea salt and black pepper. Heat the olive oil in a heavy-based casserole dish over a medium heat. Brown the poussins on all sides and remove from the casserole to a plate. Turn off the heat and leave the casserole as it is for the moment.

Combine the chopped leeks, tomatoes, pine nuts and tarragon, and mix together well. Spoon this mixture evenly into each poussin.

Reheat the casserole and put all the poussin into it. When the casserole is fairly hot, pour in the muscat or white wine, so that the pan juices are deglazed and blend with the wine. Cover and place in a moderate oven,

180°C (350°F; gas mark 4), for about 40–50 minutes, until the poussins are tender but the flesh is still slightly pink.

Remove the poussins from the casserole with a slotted spoon, put onto a serving dish and keep warm.

Put the casserole back onto the heating element and if necessary reduce the cooking juices a little. Add the cream and stir into the juices. Cook on a fast heat until the sauce has thickened slightly. Pour over the poussins and garnish with fresh sprigs of tarragon.

SPRING LAMB CASSEROLE WITH NEW SEASON VEGETABLES

NAVARIN D'AGNEAU PRINTANIER

There is nothing nicer at the start of the new season, after a long hard winter, than a tasty piece of spring lamb with young, sweet vegetables. The first time we tasted this delicious combination in France was at a nearby *ferme auberge* where the cooking is just like real home-cooking, not a commercial sauce in sight. Two courses preceded the main, though for the life of me I cannot remember what they were. It was the navarin of lamb that took all of my interest, served simply in its own juices, amidst a colourful array of spring vegetables. This is an expensive dish to prepare in France as lamb, like beef, is pricey. The tender young peas, beans and carrots are not always cheap either, but the end result is well worth the cost. A superb way to appreciate fine, fresh produce.

SERVES 4

900 g (2 lb) BONED SHOULDER OF LAMB, CUT INTO 5-cm (2-inch) PIECES
3 TABLESPOONS MILD OLIVE OIL OR SUNFLOWER OIL
SALT AND PEPPER
PINCH OF SUGAR
1 MEDIUM ONION, COARSELY CHOPPED
1 CARROT, SLICED
3 TABLESPOONS FLOUR
1 LITRE (2 PINTS) BEEF STOCK
1 CUP TOMATOES, SKINNED, SEEDED, AND CHOPPED (CANNED WILL DO)
150 ml (5 fl oz) DRY WHITE WINE
2 CLOVES GARLIC, CRUSHED
1 TEASPOON COARSELY CHOPPED FRESH ROSEMARY
1 TEASPOON FRESH THYME LEAVES
1 BAY LEAF
250 g (9 oz) SMALL WHITE ONIONS, PEELED
250 g (9 oz) SMALL BABY CARROTS, PEELED AND TRIMMED
250 g (9 oz) SMALL NEW POTATOES, SCRUBBED
250 g (9 oz) NEW PEAS, PODDED

In a cast-iron casserole, heat the oil over a medium heat until quite hot. Add the lamb and brown on all sides. Season with salt and pepper, and add a pinch of sugar to caramelise and colour the sauce. Remove the lamb to a plate using a slotted spoon, and put to one side.

Add the onion and carrot to the oil and cook for about 3 minutes, stirring now and then. Put the meat back into the casserole with the onion and carrot, and add the flour, stirring so that it does not stick. Add the stock, tomatoes, wine, garlic and herbs and bring to the boil. Reduce the heat, cover and simmer slowly for approximately 1–1¹/₂ hours, until the meat is tender.

Again remove the lamb from the casserole to a side dish. Skim any fat from the surface of the cooking juices and reduce the liquid over a high heat if need be, until the sauce has thickened slightly. Return the lamb to the casserole for the last time, and add the small onions, baby carrots and potatoes, and simmer for 10 minutes. Finally, add the peas and simmer for 5 minutes longer, until all the spring vegetables are tender.

Serve with a sprinkling of freshly chopped herbs or parsley, and a large bowl of turnips.

RAGOUT OF LAMB WITH ARTICHOKES

RAGOÛT D'AGNEAU AUX ARTICHAUTS

A hearty casserole, whose gutsy flavours are achieved by amalgamating quality produce with some simple slow cooking. It is the kind of dish you will find bubbling away in many southern farmhouse kitchens, filling the house with delicious aromas, and always ready to be eaten at midday, which is still, even in these modern times, when the main meal of the day is taken. Choose boned neck chops for this casserole.

SERVES 6

1.25 kg (2 lb 12 oz) LAMB, CUT INTO PIECES
3 TABLESPOONS OLIVE OIL
3 ONIONS, SLICED
6 POTATOES, PEELED AND CUT INTO QUARTERS
1 GOOD SPRIG THYME
SALT AND PEPPER
600 ml (20 fl oz) BEEF STOCK
6 ARTICHOKE HEARTS

Heat the olive oil in a cast-iron or heavy-based, flameproof casserole and brown the meat and onions separately. Return both to the casserole, add a little water, about 125 ml (4 fl oz), cover and cook on a low heat for approximately 15 minutes.

Add the potatoes and thyme, and season with pepper and salt. Cover the contents of the casserole with stock and simmer for 2 hours.

Add the fresh artichoke hearts 30 minutes before serving or, if they are canned, 5 minutes before serving. Serve with steamed couscous or fresh vegetables.

GREEN SALAD

SALADE VERTE

A fresh green salad makes a marvellous accompaniment to any meal, be it eaten before the main course, after or with cheese. The French are masters at making a separate course of green salad — often, the simpler the better. They are a perfect way to rest the palate and create a division between one set of flavours and the next, but are still interesting with the multitude of salad varieties and dressing combinations. For the more delicate salad varieties, choose delicate oil and vinegar combinations, such as a light olive or grape-seed oil, and tarragon or rose vinegar. For sharper tasting greens, especially the coarser winter varieties, try experimenting with walnut and other nut oils and stronger vinegars like balsamic, shallot and sherry.

SERVES 4

ANY GREEN LETTUCE OTHER THAN ICEBERG, OR A MIXTURE OF SALAD GREENS, WASHED AND DRIED — AS A GENERAL RULE, BITTER GREENS FOR WINTER, SWEETER FOR SUMMER
2 SHALLOTS, FINELY CHOPPED
OR
1 CLOVE GARLIC, CRUSHED

DRESSING

4 TABLESPOONS OLIVE OIL
2 TABLESPOONS PIQUANT RED-WINE VINEGAR
PINCH OF SUGAR
SEA SALT AND PEPPER, FRESHLY GROUND

VERSION 1

Place the salad greens in a large bowl, sprinkle the finely chopped shallots over the leaves, add the dressing and toss gently.

VERSION 2

Crush the garlic into the salad dressing and leave to steep for at least 30 minutes. If you do not have the time for this, crush the garlic into the salad bowl and rub the surface of the bowl thoroughly, leaving the bits of garlic in the bowl. Place the cleaned and dried salad greens in the bowl, add the dressing and toss gently.

This version is ideal eaten with a platter of ripened cheeses.

BROAD BEANS WITH TOMATO

FÈVES À LA TOMATE

This is another vegetable that I rush to the market for, with my basket at the ready. We can buy fresh broad beans at other times of the year too, but they are never as good as the real spring thing. Have patience with the shelling; as always it is worth the trouble.

SERVES 4

1 kg (2 lb 4 oz) UNSHELLED BROAD BEANS
SALT AND PEPPER TO TASTE
1 VERY SMALL CLOVE GARLIC, CRUSHED
1 BUNCH FLAT-LEAFED PARSLEY
2–3 TOMATOES, SKINNED AND CHOPPED

Shell the broad beans, place in a saucepan and just cover with water. Bring to the boil, salt, and add the crushed garlic to the water. Cook for approximately 15 minutes, until they are nicely al dente.

While the beans are cooking, chop the flat-leafed parsley and combine this with the chopped tomatoes. Leave the mixture to steep for 5–10 minutes.

When the beans are cooked, drain and turn out into a serving dish. Pour over the tomato and parsley mixture and season generously with freshly ground black pepper and sea salt.

BROAD BEAN CASSEROLE

FABADA

This tangy bean casserole seems to have wandered across the border with the many Spanish who over the years have settled in this region. Although the type of beans and meats differ from a true white haricot bean cassoulet, the principle and style of this dish are basically the same.

SERVES 4

300 g (10 oz) BOUDIN NOIR (BLACK SAUSAGE)
400 g (14 oz) BEST-QUALITY CHORIZO SAUSAGE
450 g (1 lb) SHOULDER OR BREAST OF PORK, GRILLED
AND CUT INTO PIECES
1 TABLESPOON DUCK FAT
1 MEDIUM ONION, PEELED AND DICED
1 kg (2 lb 3 oz) BROAD BEANS
1 TABLESPOON TOMATO CONCENTRATE
3 CLOVES GARLIC
2 GENEROUS SPRIGS FRESH THYME
1/2 TEASPOON CHILLI POWDER, OR HALF A CHILLI,
SEEDED AND CHOPPED

Peel the sausages and cut them into rounds about 2 cm (1 inch) thick. Heat the duck fat in a cast-iron casserole dish and brown the onion and the pieces of black sausage. Using a slotted spoon, transfer these to a bowl, and put on one side for the moment.

Add the broad beans to the casserole and cover with cold water. Raise the heat, add the tomato concentrate, garlic, thyme, pork, chilli, chorizo sausage and onions. Bring to the boil, stirring now and then, then reduce the heat to a steady simmer, and cook for 45–60 minutes uncovered. As the liquid reduces, you will be left with a delicious sauce.

Five minutes before serving add the black sausage, so it heats through. Serve steaming hot in shallow bowls, with crusty wholemeal bread and a glass of light red wine.

NOTE: Frozen broad beans are fine for this recipe, but take care when cooking that they do not turn mushy.

FRUITS PRESERVED IN ALCOHOL

CONFITURE DU VIEUX GARÇON

This is a method of preserving in alcohol the fruits — such as cherries, strawberries, raspberries, apricots, peaches — harvested through the year. Traditionally you served this dish at Christmas and New Year when fresh fruits were not available, as a celebration of the year's abundance.

You will need an alcohol at around 45% proof, preferably without much taste as this can affect the taste of the fruit. In France you can buy from the chemist alcohol at 90% proof which you then dilute 1:1 with water. Or you can buy a special preserving alcohol at the supermarket, or use a white rum.

Use a stoneware jar (2.5 litres) with a lid, and a small plate or saucer to keep the fruit submerged in the alcohol. Any fruit which remains uncovered could perish and taint the whole jar.

You may notice some evaporation of alcohol during the year, in which case just replace as necessary.

RIPE FRUIT IN SEASON
PRESERVING ALCOHOL
225 g (8 oz) SUGAR

Pour the alcohol into the clean jar, and dissolve the sugar. As the fruits of each season ripen, add a layer to the jar. They may tend to float, so use a saucer or small plate to keep the fruit submerged. Add more alcohol and sugar as required, allowing sufficient depth for the fruit to be always under the surface of the alcohol. Leave for at least 2–3 months before eating.

Serve with a little fresh cream or as the basis of a trifle.

WINE AND CHEESE

FROMAGE ET VIN

One of the wonderful things about France and the French, and the principal reason we came to live here, is that good eating is an essential part of the culture. It seems that every French person is an expert on food, where to find the best ingredients, how to prepare and cook them, and what wines best accompany this dish or that. This passion is shared by all, and the pleasures of past and future meals are discussed while enjoying today's.

There appear to be some rules of thumb for matching wines and dishes, but like all rules, sometimes these are hotly disputed. When the supermarkets send out their promotional wine catalogues you will always find a grid giving recommended wine and dish combinations. This advice is too important to try and trick you. Like the advice of a good sommelier, it is a privilege to be let in on the secret.

It was not until we came to live in France that we discovered the truth in the saying 'the sum is greater than the parts', particularly with respect to the marriage of cheese and wine.

Try this. Take a piece of goat cheese, like *Pélardon*, demi-sec (about a month old), put it in your mouth and hold it there. Take a sip of good red wine with a bit of body to it, like St Chinian or Faugères. Chew both together.

Enjoy the taste explosion. Life will never be the same again.

GOAT CHEESE WITH HONEY

FROMAGE DE CHÈVRE AU MIEL

A simple, satisfying way to serve fresh goat cheese. Ideally, use a small round cheese like *Pélardon*, or slices of a fresh *bûche*, or log-shaped goat cheese. They should be no older that one month, so the flavour is still fruity and sharp. Choose a strongly flavoured honey, like chestnut or acacia, but not one that is too sweet.

2 SLICES GOAT CHEESE PER PERSON
APPROXIMATELY 1 TABLESPOON HONEY
THYME FLOWERS, TO GARNISH

Slice the *Pélardon* in half and arrange on a plate. Drizzle the honey over the cheese, and garnish with thyme flowers. Serve with some fresh bread, and a glass of full-bodied red wine.

GOAT CHEESE IN OLIVE OIL

FROMAGE DE CHÈVRE À L'HUILE D'OLIVE

A rather particular southern speciality, preserved goat cheese with herbs makes a tasty quick snack when spread on warm toast or served with a crisp salad of spicy greens like roquette and frisée. Made in spring, this will keep well into the early winter if stored carefully.

FOR A 500 g (1 lb 2 oz) JAR

3 OR 4 SMALL GOAT CHEESES, ABOUT 1 MONTH OLD
SEVERAL SPRIGS EACH OF FRESH SAVORY, ROSEMARY
AND OREGANO
1 TEASPOON PEPPERCORNS
BEST-QUALITY OLIVE OIL

Wash and dry a glass preserving jar. Carefully place the cheeses in the jar and tuck in all the fresh herbs around them. Sprinkle the peppercorns into the jar, and pour in enough olive oil to completely cover the cheeses.

Leave for several weeks before using.

LEMON TART

TARTE AU CITRON

A good tarte au citron is really very hard to beat when it comes to the dessert stakes. But it must have a wonderfully rich pastry base, and the lemons you use need to be as fresh as possible. Always serve it just a few hours after it has left the oven.

FOR THE PÂTE SABLÉE (PASTRY BASE)

1 EGG
125 g (4 oz) VERY FINE CASTOR SUGAR
ZEST OF LEMON
250 g (9 oz) SIFTED PLAIN FLOUR
125 g (4 oz) CHILLED UNSALTED BUTTER
ICING SUGAR

In a spacious bowl, beat the egg and sugar together thoroughly, and add the zest of a lemon. Rub in the sifted flour, and finally knead in the butter.

Quickly work the pastry into a ball using icing sugar instead of flour to stop it sticking. Wrap in cling film and rest in the refrigerator for at least an hour.

Roll out with icing sugar when ready, and line a 25-cm (10-inch) fluted tart tin with removable base with the pastry. Bake blind in a hot oven, 200°C (400°F; gas mark 6), for 10 minutes, until golden brown.

This makes about 500 g (1 lb 2 oz) of pastry.

FOR THE CREAM

2 EGGS, BEATEN
200 g (7 oz) CASTOR SUGAR
75 g (3 oz) BUTTER, MELTED
JUICE OF 2 FRESH LEMONS

Mix the sugar into the beaten eggs thoroughly, until the mixture is pale and creamy. Stir in the melted butter and the juice of the 2 lemons.

Reduce the oven heat to 180°C (350°F; gas mark 4). Pour the creamed mixture into the pastry case and bake for 20 minutes, until the top of the tart is nicely golden but not brown. Place a piece of foil over the top if necessary. Remove from the tin while still warm and leave to cool.

Serve with a dusting of icing sugar and fresh cream.

NOTE: If you refrigerate this dessert it will not be as delicious or have as good a consistency as it would if served only just cooled from the oven.

CHERRY JAM

CONFITURE DE CERISES

Living in such a prolific fruit-growing area, we are spoilt by the abundance of fresh stone fruit from May through to September. As well as stoned fruits, we also benefit from a microclimate mild enough to grow oranges and lemons, quinces, apples and pears, even raspberries and currants. And with so many mouths to feed at breakfast, what better way to put all these fruits to use than by making jams and jellies. It is an endless task, as we find the flavour of jams is best preserved by making them in small quantities, ideally 3 kg (6 lb 10 oz) of fruit per batch of jam. Depending on the fruit, this quantity generally makes 10–12 jars of confiture. By May, the first batches of black and white cherry jam are put away in the storage cupboard, only to disappear almost as fast as it has been made. And so it goes, right through to winter, when we stock up on clementine and orange marmalades.

The basic principles are much the same for most jams; it just depends on the type of fruit, and their water and pectin contents. The most important ingredient aside from the fruit is sugar — not enough and the jam will ferment, too much and it will crystallise. As a general rule of thumb, we use kilo for kilo of fruit and sugar, and alter this to 1 kg of fruit to 800 g (1³/₄ lb) sugar in the case of high-pectin fruits like apples, plums and citrus. The juice of a few lemons, or the pips from them, often helps with low-pectin fruits.

2.25 kg (5 lb) CHERRIES, WASHED, STALKED AND STONED
JUICE OF 3 LEMONS
2.25 kg (5 lb) SUGAR

Put the cherries and lemon juice in a large jamming pan. Keep a dozen of the cherry stones, tie them in a little square of muslin or cotton, and add them to the cherries.

Cook over a gentle heat until the juice of the cherries begins to run, then raise the heat and simmer until tender. Remove the bag of stones.

Add the sugar quickly, stirring until it is dissolved, and raise the heat as rapidly as possible to a rolling boil. Keep stirring and start testing the jam for a set after 10 minutes. If you do not have a jamming thermometer, the simplest way to do this is to dribble a small amount of the mixture onto a chilled saucer. Wait for 1 minute, then run your finger through the jam. If a skin forms on top of the mixture, it is ready to pot. If not, keep boiling and test in another 5 minutes.

When the jam has reached setting point, pot in washed, warmed, sterilised jars after allowing the jam to cool slightly, and seal.

CHERRY PUDDING
CLAFOUTIS

Living as we do in a cherry-growing region, this wonderful pudding gets baked quite a lot *chez nous*. We even preserve enough cherries in the spring to see us through the winter so that we can enjoy it all year round. If cherries are hard to come by, though, it is equally delicious made with prunes, apricots, pears or plums. The more tart the fruit, the better. When it comes to stone fruits there are two differing opinions — some say to cook the fruit unstoned in the pudding as this adds to the flavour, while others find the stones bothersome and remove them prior to baking.

SERVES 4–6

75 g (3 oz) FLOUR
50 g (2 oz) SUGAR
3 EGGS
450 ml (16 fl oz) MILK
25 g (1 oz) BUTTER
450 g (1 lb) BLACK CHERRIES, STONED OR NOT
BROWN SUGAR FOR SPRINKLING ON THE TOP

Sift the flour into a mixing bowl and, making a well in the centre, add the sugar and eggs. Gently stir in the flour, and as the mixture thickens start to add the milk a little at a time. When all the milk is added beat the mixture vigorously so that you end up with a runny batter with no lumps.

Thoroughly grease a shallow, ovenproof dish with some butter. Spread the cherries over the bottom of the dish and gently pour on the batter. Dot the surface with a few knobs of butter and place in a moderately hot oven, 200°C (400°F; gas mark 6), and cook for approximately 35–45 minutes.

Five minutes before serving, sprinkle the surface of the pudding with brown sugar so that when it is ready the top is nicely browned with a fine layer of sugary crust.

Serve either hot or cold.

STRAWBERRIES IN RED WINE
FRAISES AU VIN ROUGE

This dish is best made with a highly perfumed, small variety of strawberry, and a fine Côte du Rhône style of wine. It is also excellent with a muscat dessert wine, but choose a good-quality muscat that leaves a clean, dry aftertaste on the palate, rather than cloying sweetness. A hint about choosing strawberries — if they do not smell sweet and are not highly perfumed, it is likely they will be tasteless and acidic. This could be because they have been picked before they were fully ripe. Also, there are some varieties of strawberry that are grown to look better than they taste, and will never really give that special strawberry burst of flavour that other varieties can provide.

SERVES 6

1 kg (2 lb 4 oz) RIPE STRAWBERRIES, WASHED AND HULLED
125 g (4 oz) VANILLA CASTOR SUGAR
350 ml (12 fl oz) CÔTE DU RHÔNE-STYLE RED WINE OR MUSCAT

About 30–45 minutes before you are ready to serve them, place the strawberries in a spacious glass bowl. If you are using a large variety of strawberry, you may want to halve them.

Sprinkle over the vanilla castor sugar, then pour over the wine or muscat. Stir well. Leave the strawberries to macerate in the alcohol, turning them now and again with a spoon. Serve on their own, with fresh cream, chocolate custards (see page 116) or crème anglaise (see page 125).

TRADITIONAL CARAMEL CUSTARDS

CRÈME CARAMEL

A French classic through and through. Once mastered, this recipe is very straightforward, and relatively quick and easy to prepare in advance. A baked custard will always give you a superior flavour and texture to refrigerator-set creams, and do not be put off by the bain-marie — a simple roasting pan with some water in it is all that is required.

SERVES 6

FOR THE CARAMEL

50 g (2 oz) CUBE SUGAR
A LITTLE WATER (SEVERAL TEASPOONS)
A LITTLE LEMON JUICE OR VINEGAR

Place the sugar cubes in a saucepan and dampen with water. Place the pan on a gentle heat.

When the sugar has dissolved, bring it to the boil and watch carefully, so that the caramel browns but does not burn too much and become bitter.

Shake the pan from time to time so that the caramel cooks evenly. Never stir the mixture with anything. When the caramel is the required colour (the darker it is the more bitter it will be; a nice mahogany is ideal) remove the pan from the heat.

Working quickly, pour the caramel into the base of a mould or individual ramekins, and holding the mould with a tea towel, turn it until it is coated with caramel. Leave to cool.

FOR THE CUSTARD

500 ml (16 fl oz) MILK
1 VANILLA POD FOR FLAVOURING
75 g (3 oz) CASTOR SUGAR
3 WHOLE EGGS

Boil the milk in a saucepan with the split vanilla pod. Add the sugar and stir. Once the milk has boiled, leave it to stand for 5 minutes before removing the vanilla pod.

In a separate bowl, whisk the eggs rapidly with a fork or mixer. Gently, a little at a time, add the hot milk to the beaten eggs, stirring continuously. The slower the better, as you do not want the eggs to curdle. Proceed until all the milk and egg is combined.

Pour into the caramelised mould or moulds, place in a bain-marie or water bath, and cook gently in a preheated oven at 160°C (325°F; gas mark 3). Allow 1–1½ hours. The cooking time will vary according to the size of your mould.

Small ramekins and metal moulds will cook more quickly than a large mould but the most important thing is to make sure that the water in the bain-marie never boils. Slow and steady is ideal. To test if cooked, press your fingertip lightly onto the centre of the cream. It should be slightly resistant to the touch.

Once the crème caramel is cooked, remove from the oven and the bain-marie, and leave to cool completely. Refrigerate for the last hour.

Once completely cold, run the point of a knife carefully around the edges to loosen the dessert. To remove the crème caramel from the mould, place a serving dish over the mould and turn it upside-down quickly. When the crème is detached from the mould, remove the mould carefully and serve.

NOTE: This recipe can also be used to make a large flan in a fluted metal mould. Make the caramel in the mould itself and follow the recipe above for the crème.

SUMMER

SÈTE FISH SOUP

BOURRIDE

A native of Sète, a large fishing port on the southern French coast of the Mediterranean, this fish soup is traditionally made with monkfish. A plainly ugly creature, its flesh is firm, white and delicious, not unlike that of sea bass or New Zealand hapuku. However, you can use other fish varieties like snapper, bream, grey or red mullet or John Dory if you like. As with the famous bouillabaisse, you will not need anything else before or after, as it is a meal in itself.

SERVES 6

1 kg (2 lb 4 oz) FIRM WHITE FISH, CLEANED, FILLETED AND CUT INTO THICK SLICES
CARCASSES AND HEADS OF THE FISH
1 LITRE (2 PINTS) WATER
200 ml (7 fl oz) WHITE WINE
THE WHITE OF A LEEK, CHOPPED INTO ROUNDS
1 ONION, GRATED
1 CARROT, CHOPPED INTO ROUNDS
1 CLOVE GARLIC, FLATTENED UNDER THE BLADE OF A KNIFE
A PIECE OF ORANGE PEEL ABOUT 2 cm x 2 cm (1 inch x 1 inch)
SALT AND PEPPER TO SEASON
AÏOLI (SEE PAGE 36)
3–4 EGG YOLKS
30 ml (1 fl oz) CREAM
TOASTED BAGUETTE

In a stockpot, put the water, wine, the heads and carcasses of the fish, leek, onion, carrot, garlic, orange peel and seasoning. Bring to the boil and cook for 5–10 minutes. Reduce the heat slightly and poach the fish pieces for 12–15 minutes, or until just cooked. Lift the fish out with a slotted spoon and place in a deep serving dish; put to one side, keeping it warm.

Divide the aïoli mixture in two and put one portion aside to serve with the bourride. To the other half, add the egg yolks and cream and stir thoroughly.

Drain the stock and discard the bones and vegetables.

Rinse the pot, pour the stock back into it, and return it to the stove on the lowest heat possible. To the aïoli, cream and egg mixture, add a few spoonfuls of fish stock stirring continuously. Then slowly, little by little, add this mixture to the fish stock in the pot. Continue stirring with a wooden spoon until the sauce coats the back of the spoon and the soup is smooth and creamy. Under no circumstances allow the soup to boil as it will curdle in a matter of moments.

Return the pieces of poached fish to the soup, and serve in deep, wide bowls with the aïoli spread on toasted baguette rounds floating on top, and a large bowl of boiled potatoes.

COLD FENNEL AND TOMATO SOUP

SOUPE GLACÉE AU FENOUIL ET À LA TOMATE

A refreshing, tangy soup for those hot, balmy evenings when appetites are light. And if you feel that cold soups should be a bit spicy, serve it with a bowl of Harissa (see page 125) on the side, so your guests can please themselves.

SERVES 4

500 g (1 lb 2 oz) RIPE TOMATOES
2 LARGE FENNEL BULBS, CLEANED, TRIMMED AND CUT INTO QUARTERS
1 HEAPED TEASPOON COARSE-GRAINED SEA SALT
1/2 TEASPOON PEPPERCORNS
1 TEASPOON YELLOW MUSTARD SEEDS
1 TEASPOON CORIANDER SEEDS
2 TABLESPOONS FIRST-PRESSING OLIVE OIL
1 SMALL ONION, CHOPPED
2 LARGE CLOVES GARLIC, CRUSHED
1 TABLESPOON BALSAMIC VINEGAR
1 TABLESPOON LEMON JUICE
1 TEASPOON CHOPPED FRESH CHERVIL
FRESH CHERVIL, CORIANDER OR FENNEL FRONDS TO GARNISH

First of all, skin the tomatoes. To do this, pour enough boiling water over the tomatoes to cover them, and leave for about 1 minute, no longer. Drain them and run them under cold water — the skins will peel off easily. Chop the tomatoes roughly.

Place the fennel in a saucepan with 450 ml (14 fl oz) of cold water, add the salt and bring to the boil, then simmer for 10 minutes.

In a mortar and pestle or food processor, crush the peppercorns, mustard and coriander seeds.

Heat the oil in a large saucepan and add the crushed spices and chopped onion. Cook for about 5 minutes, stirring occasionally, then add the crushed garlic and continue to cook for a few more minutes. Add the balsamic vinegar, lemon juice, chopped tomatoes and chervil. Combine the ingredients well, and finally add the cooked fennel and the water that it is cooked in. Cook for a further 30 minutes on a low heat, stirring now and then.

Allow the soup to cool, then purée. Pour into a soup tureen and chill for a few hours in the refrigerator. Garnish with fresh herbs and serve with Tomato and Garlic Bread (see page 34).

SAUTÉED SHRIMPS

CREVETTES SAUTÉES

The very first night I ever set foot in France, we chose this dish for an entrée. It was in a funny little restaurant in the heart of Normandy, almost empty of diners, with the television blaring out the current soccer match in one corner. There was little need for concern, however, because when our shrimps arrived in a hot sizzling mound, they were the freshest, sweetest things I had ever tasted. For this dish to be really stunning, the shrimps need to be caught the day you cook them.

SERVES 6

500 g (1 lb 2 oz) GREY SHRIMPS, VERY FRESH
4 TABLESPOONS OLIVE OIL
FRESHLY GROUND SEA SALT AND BLACK PEPPER

Heat the olive oil in a large frying pan until it begins to smoke. Tip the shrimps straight into the pan and quickly cover with a lid so that they do not pop over the side. Shake the pan vigorously at the same time and leave covered for 1 minute. Remove the lid and turn the shrimps with a wooden spatula until they have changed to a rose colour.

Sprinkle with salt and pepper and serve immediately with brown bread.

TOMATO AND GARLIC BREAD

PAIN GRILLÉ À LA TOMATE ET À L'AIL

With the Spanish border only an hour away, the region cannot help but be influenced by the culture, hence the Spanish-sounding names and bull-fighting traditions that are found between Arles and Perpignan today.

We can easily go for the day or a long weekend to enjoy tasty seafood and light Spanish wines. That is how we came across this wonderful toast that goes with so many summer dishes.

PAIN DE CAMPAGNE, ESPECIALLY GOOD FOR MAKING TOMATO AND GARLIC BREAD

SERVES 4

2 ROUNDS OF TOASTED WHOLEMEAL BREAD PER PERSON
3–4 CLOVES OF GARLIC, PEELED AND LEFT WHOLE
A SMALL BOTTLE OF FIRST-PRESSING OLIVE OIL
SEVERAL RIPE TOMATOES, CUT INTO QUARTERS
COARSE-GRAINED SEA SALT AND BLACK PEPPER TO GRIND OVER THE TOP

Take a round of toasted bread and rub the surface with a clove of garlic, then rub the surface with a piece of tomato. Drizzle some olive oil over the surface, and then freshly milled pepper and salt.

Serve with slices of finely sliced dried ham like Serrano or Parma ham, or serve as an accompaniment to soups and entrées.

The bread can be prepared in advance but it will go soggy after 5 or 10 minutes.

ONION AND OLIVE BREAD

FOUACE

This is the French version of focaccia bread, most commonly found in the Midi. In Provence it is called fougasse. Although less common in northern France, various regions still produce their own sweet and savoury varieties. Like focaccia, it makes an ideal summer festive bread to serve with a simple barbecue of vine-grilled poultry, red meats and fresh salads. The onion and olive filling is our favourite but can easily be replaced with a myriad of other combinations, limited only by your own imagination.

FOR THE FILLING

2–3 TABLESPOONS OLIVE OIL
2–3 MEDIUM-SIZED ONIONS, SLICED
2 CLOVES GARLIC, PEELED AND CRUSHED
3 BRANCHES FRESH THYME
3 TABLESPOONS BROWN SUGAR
2 HANDFULS BLACK OLIVES, PITTED AND CHOPPED

Pour the olive oil into a heavy-bottomed cast-iron pan over a medium heat, and braise the onions, garlic and thyme. Add the brown sugar and mix in to allow the mixture to caramelise a little. When most of the juice has evaporated, add the olives and mix well together.

FOR THE DOUGH

1 PACKET DRIED YEAST
1 TEASPOON HONEY
150 ml (5 fl oz) WARM WATER

700 g (1 lb 8 oz) WHITE FLOUR
1 TEASPOON SALT
350 ml (12 fl oz) WARM WATER

First make the starter by placing the dried yeast and honey in a small bowl and pouring over the warm water. Stir then cover with a linen tea towel. Place in a warm, dry, draught-free place for 10 minutes, or until the yeast is bubbling and expanding. A hot-water cupboard is ideal.

Sift the flour and add the salt, mixing it with the flour. When the starter is ready, make a well in the centre of the flour and pour the starter into the centre of the well, mixing with a knife. Then add the rest of the warm water until the mixture is moist but not too wet. (You may not need all the water, depending on the quality of the flour you use.) Discard the knife and turn the dough out on to a clean board or table. Start kneading the dough with the heel of your palm, sprinkling more flour over the dough if necessary to stop it sticking to the surface. When the dough is evenly worked and smooth, roll it out roughly, keeping it reasonably thick but wide enough to take the onion mixture inside, and fold in half again.

TO MAKE UP

Spread the onion and olive filling evenly over one half of the dough. Make sure the layer is not too thick as this will leave the dough next to the onions soft and disagreeable in texture when cooked.

Fold over the top layer and, taking a large knife, make several incisions on the top, to allow the air to escape while the bread is cooking. Organise the edges so that the bread is roughly oval in shape. Sprinkle the top with a little coarse sea salt if you wish.

Place on an oiled oven tray, cover with a linen tea towel, and rest the bread in a warm, dry and draught-free place for about an hour, until it has almost doubled in size.

Cook in a hot oven, 230°C (450°F; gas mark 8), for about 20–25 minutes, until golden brown. The bottom of the bread should sound hollow when you tap it.

Place on an oven rack to cool so that the air can pass underneath the bread, allowing the base to stay crisp.

GARLIC MAYONNAISE
AÏOLI

An essential addition to any cook's repertoire, this wonderful Provençal concoction accompanies classic French fish dishes like Bourride (see page 32), a white fish soup, poached salt cod, as well as hard-boiled eggs, crudités and cold meats. It holds the force of the strongest Midi summer's day, is straightforward and quick to create, so what could be better? Use fresh egg yolks at room temperature and a first-pressing olive oil that is good and fruity, also at room temperature.

SERVES 8

2 LARGE CLOVES GARLIC, PEELED
3 EGG YOLKS
500 ml (1 pint) APPROX OF FIRST-PRESSING OLIVE OIL
PINCH OF SALT
JUICE OF A LEMON

In a large mortar, crush the garlic with the pestle until it is the consistency of pulp. This will take about 5 minutes. Add the egg yolks and a pinch of salt, and stir with a wooden spoon until all these ingredients are well amalgamated.

Start adding the olive oil, very slowly at first, practically drop by drop, stirring all the while, until the Aïoli starts to thicken. When you have used about half the oil, you can start to add the oil in a slow and steady stream. The mixture will get thicker and thicker, which is what you want. Add a dash of lemon juice right at the end and serve in the mortar or in a comfortable mound in an earthenware serving dish.

If your Aïoli begins to separate, this is usually because the oil has been added too quickly. To reconstitute the mixture, put an egg yolk in another bowl, and slowly add the curdled mixture to it.

This recipe will make enough aïoli for 8 people with poached fish and vegetables. To make a smaller quantity, use 2 cloves of garlic, 1 egg yolk and about 150 ml (5 fl oz) of olive oil.

ANCHOVY PÂTÉ
ANCHOÏADE

Anchoïade is one of those wholly distinctive Midi dishes. We would never think of eating it at any other time but summer — preferably when the main heat of the day has passed, in the shade of the terrace, with good friends and a fine glass of white or rosé wine to accompany it.

SERVES 4

350 g (12 oz) ANCHOVY FILLETS.
3 CLOVES GARLIC, CRUSHED
200 ml (7 fl oz) OLIVE OIL
1 TABLESPOON VINEGAR
GROUND BLACK PEPPER

If the anchovy fillets are preserved in salt, make sure they are washed and drained of salt; the easiest way is to soak them in cold water for an hour, then wipe with a paper towel.

METHOD A

Place all the ingredients in a food processor. Mix well to a smooth paste, and serve.

METHOD B

Place the garlic and anchovies in a mortar and crush with the pestle. Add the ground black pepper and stir in the vinegar. Then add the oil little by little as you go. Work steadily until all the oil is absorbed and the mixture is the consistency of a smooth paste.

Turn out into a shallow bowl and serve in the late summer sun with crudités and warm rye bread.

RED CAPSICUM PESTO
PESTO AUX POIVRONS ROUGES

In the summer months pestos make delicious pre-dinner nibbles, spread over home-made breads or toasted baguette. Usually it is made with fresh herbs, ground to a paste, but we were inspired by the massive quantities of sweet peppers grown here to try making it with roasted red peppers. The outcome was very tasty. For a colourful entrée, arrange a generous dob of Tapenade (see opposite) and Red Capsicum Pesto on a flat plate, with some young roquette. Serve drizzled with a little nutty olive oil, lots of freshly ground black pepper and toasted rye bread. Other pestos to try are roasted aubergine, sun-dried tomato, chervil, coriander, flat-leafed parsley and roquette.

MAKES APPROXIMATELY 300 g

2–3 MEDIUM-SIZED, ROASTED RED PEPPERS, SEEDED AND SKINNED
75 g (3 oz) PINE NUTS, ROASTED
2 CLOVES GARLIC
30 g (1 oz) PARMESAN, FRESHLY GRATED
50 ml (2 fl oz) FIRST-PRESSING OLIVE OIL

In a food processor or blender, combine the peppers, pine nuts and garlic. Process these into a paste, then add the parmesan and finally drizzle in the olive oil, until you have achieved a pliable paste consistency. Take care not to add too much oil.

NOTE: When making herb pestos, allow 2 good bunches of herb leaves. The amount of garlic can be altered according to individual taste.

OLIVE PÂTÉ
TAPENADE

A standard Provençal favourite, but no summer is complete without its fair share of tapenade consumption. We seem to make kilos of the stuff throughout the hot dry months and smear it on whatever is going. A Parisienne friend recently introduced us to raw courgettes stuffed with tapenade as an hors d'oeuvre. Tapenade goes remarkably well with a roasted tomato confiture and roasted leg of lamb, not to mention a good chunk of freshly baked rye bread. This is a particularly good recipe and stores well in an airtight jar for 2–3 weeks.

250 g (9 oz) BLACK OLIVES, STONED
100 g (3 oz) CANNED ANCHOVY FILLETS, DRAINED
100 g (3 oz) CANNED TUNA, DRAINED
100 g (3 oz) CAPERS, DRAINED
1 SPRIG FRESH THYME
1 BAY LEAF
2 LARGE CLOVES GARLIC, PEELED
1 SMALL GLASS EAU-DE-VIE OR COGNAC
4 TABLESPOONS OLIVE OIL
GROUND BLACK PEPPER, TO TASTE

Place all the ingredients except the olive oil in a food processor, and at a slow speed mix to give a chunky consistency. Slowly pour in the olive oil. If you want a very smooth pâté, let the food processor run a bit longer. Season with pepper, turn out and leave to rest for an hour or so before serving.

Always serve at room temperature, with vegetables, wholemeal bread or baguette and a glass of chilled wine.

To serve as an hors d'oeuvre with courgettes, take 2 or 3 fresh, medium-sized courgettes and halve lengthways. Scrape out the seeds with a teaspoon and refill the cavity with tapenade. Cut into bite-size pieces, *et voila*!

MARINATED SARDINES

SARDINES MARINÉES

Between May and August our mobile fishmonger always has a good supply of fresh sardines. So on Friday, which is market day in our village, we often serve them simply in their marinade, accompanied by some crusty bread and a glass of chilled Picpoul de Pinet, a crisp white wine from the region. If you cannot get hold of sardines the next best thing is very fresh sprats, the smaller the better. If you have not caught the fish yourself, the freshness is best judged by their fresh seaweedy smell, firm elastic flesh and damp bright-red gills.

SERVES 4

500 g (1 lb 2 oz) VERY FRESH SARDINES OR SPRATS
JUICE OF 2–3 LEMONS
75–125 ml (3–4 fl oz) FIRST-PRESSING OLIVE OIL
SALT AND PEPPER TO SEASON
2 LARGE CLOVES GARLIC, CRUSHED
2 TABLESPOONS CHOPPED FLAT-LEAFED PARSLEY
1 TEASPOON FINELY CHOPPED FRESH OREGANO,

Wash and scale the sardines or sprats. Now fillet the fish, one by one. Laying the fish on its side on a board and with a very sharp knife, almost at the same angle as the fish, make a small incision just below the head and gills. With your left hand, press firmly but lightly on the fish and slide the knife down the length of the fish, finishing at the tail. Repeat on the other side. Keep the

bones and head for the cat. Wash the fillets thoroughly and check that there are no stray scales left. Leave the fillets to drain and pat them dry with paper towels.

Make up the dressing by whisking together the freshly squeezed lemon juice and the olive oil. Season with freshly ground coarse sea salt and black pepper. Add the crushed garlic, parsley and oregano.

Choose a shallow glass or earthenware dish, spoon some of the dressing into the dish, put a layer of fish on top, spoon on some more dressing, make another layer of fish, and so on. Continue this way until all the fish is in the dish and is fully immersed by the dressing. Leave to pickle in a cool place for 2–3 hours, checking from time to time to make sure they are turning whitish as the pickling process takes place. They can be refrigerated like this for up to 24 hours.

To serve, create an elegant mound of the fish on individual serving plates and spoon over the dressing.

LITTLE SQUID IN WHITE WINE

SÉPIONS AU VIN BLANC

With the fishing port of Sète only an hour away, there is always an abundance of fresh fish readily available. The variety of fish you can find in the markets is amazing, and the big supermarkets regard their extensive fish counters with pride. We pick the small squid (sépions) for this dish, and a good dry white wine — Picpoul de Pinet is the Muscadet of the Languedoc.

Ask your fishmonger to clean and skin the squid.

SERVES 4

600 g (1 lb 4 oz) SÉPIONS (LITTLE SQUID), CLEANED AND SKINNED.
2 TABLESPOONS OLIVE OIL
2–3 CLOVES GARLIC, COARSELY CHOPPED
1 GLASS (150 ml) DRY WHITE WINE
GROUND BLACK PEPPER AND SALT, TO TASTE
1–2 TEASPOONS CHOPPED PARSLEY,

Heat the oil in a frying pan to a high heat, add the garlic and cook for 1–2 minutes, until just starting to brown. Still on a high heat, add the little squid, stirring quickly so that they do not stick to the pan, and cook for 2–3 minutes. Add the white wine, and reduce the heat to a simmer. The squid will only require 4–5 minutes' cooking in total.

When they are tender and just cooked, season with pepper and salt, and serve with a sprinkling of parsley.

PEPPERS WITH ANCHOVIES

POIVRONS AUX ANCHOIS

We are die-hard fans of pepper (capsicum) dishes, and are always looking out for new recipes. We love cooking them and experiencing the fantastic explosion of tastes in the mouth, and the colours — red, green, yellow — look spectacular. The process of removing the skin is a bit of a nuisance, but the effort is well worth it. Left in place, the skin always retains a certain bitterness, while roasted and peeled, peppers have that caramelised melt-in-the mouth sweetness.

<u>SERVES 4</u>

2–3 PEPPERS, RED, GREEN AND YELLOW
4 ANCHOVY FILLETS, CHOPPED COARSELY
1 TABLESPOON CAPERS, FINELY CHOPPED
1 TABLESPOON FINELY CHOPPED, FRESH OREGANO
1 CLOVE GARLIC, FINELY CHOPPED
GROUND BLACK PEPPER, TO TASTE
6 TABLESPOONS OLIVE OIL

To remove the pepper skins, after first removing the stems and seeds: either put the peppers on a baking tray under a very hot grill, turning to expose a new face when the skin chars, or hold the pepper in metal tongs over a high gas flame, turning the pepper to char all the skin. Once charred, put the peppers in a plastic bag, seal the opening and leave for 5–10 minutes. Take out of the bag and remove the skin, which will come away easily.

Cut the peppers in half and then into thin strips, and place in the bottom of a flat serving dish. Spread over the anchovies, capers, oregano, garlic and black pepper. Drizzle over the olive oil. Allow to marinate for at least 2 hours, stirring occasionally. Serve on individual dishes in a colourful mound, with the marinade spooned over the peppers.

PEPPERS WITH CAPERS AND OLIVES

POIVRONS AUX CÂPRES ET AUX OLIVES

SERVES 4

3–4 PEPPERS, RED, GREEN AND YELLOW
3–4 TABLESPOONS OLIVE OIL
2–3 CLOVES GARLIC, CRUSHED
2 TABLESPOONS BLACK OLIVES, PITTED
2 TABLESPOONS CAPERS
GROUND BLACK PEPPER AND SALT, TO TASTE

Remove the stems and seeds from the peppers and cut them into quarters.

In a large frying pan, heat the olive oil to a low-medium heat, add the garlic and sauté gently until golden. Add the peppers and sauté for 10 minutes, stirring occasionally.

Add the olives and capers and simmer for a further 15 minutes. Season. Remove from the heat and cool before serving.

ROASTED PEPPER SALAD

SALADE DE POIVRONS ROTIS

SERVES 4

3–4 PEPPERS, RED, GREEN AND YELLOW
1 CLOVE GARLIC, SLICED
1 TABLESPOON CHOPPED PARSLEY
4 TABLESPOONS OLIVE OIL
GROUND SEA SALT, TO TASTE

Remove the stems and seeds from the peppers, and roast them until tender. Leave to cool before removing the skins, then cut the peppers into strips.

Put the pepper strips, garlic, parsley and olive oil in a salad bowl. Season and stir well. Allow to stand for at least 2 hours to allow the flavours to develop.

PEPPERS IN BALSAMIC VINEGAR

POIVRONS AU VINAIGRE BALSAMIQUE

SERVES 4

2–3 PEPPERS
3 TABLESPOONS OLIVE OIL
2 CLOVES GARLIC, CRUSHED
GROUND BLACK PEPPER AND SALT, TO TASTE
1 TABLESPOON BALSAMIC VINEGAR

Remove the stems and seeds from the peppers and cut them into strips.

Heat the oil in a frying pan to a high heat, add the peppers and fry rapidly until the edges start to brown, turning from time to time to avoid burning. Add the garlic, allowing it to cook for a few minutes.

Still on a high heat, add the seasoning and the vinegar. Stir until the vinegar has almost evaporated. Serve.

PROVENÇAL TOMATOES

TOMATES À LA PROVENÇALE

With all the full flavours of the Mediterranean sunshine, sun-ripened tomatoes, a sprinkling of fresh herbs, garlic and a splash of fruity olive oil, this dish makes a mouthwatering start to any al fresco dinner. It is also a delicious companion to barbecued meats, especially chicken.

SERVES 4

6 MEDIUM SUN-RIPENED TOMATOES, WASHED AND DRIED
50 ml (2 fl oz) FRUITY OLIVE OIL
1 TABLESPOON BROWN SUGAR
3 CLOVES GARLIC, PEELED AND FINELY CHOPPED
2 TABLESPOONS CHOPPED FLAT-LEAFED PARSLEY, BASIL, CHERVIL OR TARRAGON

Cut the tomatoes in half and spoon out the seeds. Heat a little of the olive oil in a heavy-bottomed frying pan, place the tomatoes in the pan, face down, and cook on a very gentle heat for 10 minutes. Turn them over carefully.

Into each tomato half put a sprinkling of sugar, garlic, chopped herbs and a drizzle of olive oil. Leave them to cook for another 10–15 minutes, spooning the juices that escape back into the halves every now and then. Leave to cool.

Carefully arrange 3 tomato halves per person on 4 individual plates, spoon over the cooking juices, and add a little freshly ground black pepper. Serve with chunks of nutty rye bread.

HOT GOAT CHEESE SALAD WITH HERBS

SALADE AU FROMAGE DE CHÈVRE CHAUD

In the south of France this hot salad is an institution. In the summer months it is hard to find a restaurant menu without it. Sadly, not all that you find are pleasing to the palate, but with the right ingredients, a good goat cheese being essential, it is hard to go wrong with this southern classic. The ideal goat cheese is one that has been ripened for about a month.

SERVES 4

4 SMALL GOAT CHEESES OR A LOG-SHAPED GOAT CHEESE, SLICED
2 TABLESPOONS OLIVE OIL
1 OAK-LEAF LETTUCE, WASHED AND DRIED
1 BUNCH CRESS, WASHED AND DRIED
8 ROUNDS BAGUETTE, LIGHTLY TOASTED

FOR THE DRESSING

2 TABLESPOONS WALNUT OIL
2 TABLESPOONS MILD OLIVE OIL OR SUNFLOWER OIL
2 TABLESPOONS WINE VINEGAR
PINCH OF SUGAR
FRESHLY GROUND SEA SALT AND PEPPER
1 TEASPOON EACH FINELY CHOPPED FLAT-LEAFED PARSLEY, CHERVIL, TARRAGON AND CHIVES

Brush the goat cheeses all over with olive oil about 1–2 hours beforehand and leave to rest in a cool, dry place.

Combine the salad greens and dress with the herb dressing. Arrange evenly on 4 salad plates. Cut the cheeses in half, so you have 2 slices of cheese per person.

Place the cheese on top of the toasted baguette rounds, and grill under a high heat for about 5 minutes, or until the cheese is melting.

Place the cheese and croûtons in the centre of each salad and sprinkle with some freshly ground pepper. Serve straight away, while still hot.

BRAISED FENNEL IN BALSAMIC VINEGAR

FENOUIL BRAISÉ AU VINAIGRE BALSAMIQUE

In southern France, fresh fennel bulbs are available practically all year round. But their slightly aniseed flavour is at its best in late spring and summer.

This dish is very easy to prepare and makes a refreshing entrée, served cold at the height of summer.

SERVES 4

4 FENNEL BULBS, TRIMMED AND WASHED
3 TABLESPOONS OLIVE OIL
50 ml (2 fl oz) BALSAMIC VINEGAR
GROUND SEA SALT AND PEPPER TO SEASON
SEVERAL STEMS FRESH CHERVIL, CHOPPED, OR THE
FEATHERY TOPS FROM THE BULBS, TO GARNISH

Split the fennel bulbs in two with a sharp knife so that each half will lie flat. In a heavy-bottomed, cast-iron frying pan, warm the olive oil and place the fennel bulbs flat-side down in the pan. Cover and slowly cook each side for about 15–20 minutes. The cooking time will depend on the size of the fennel bulbs. If necessary add a little water and more oil so that they do not burn. When the fennel is almost cooked it will look slightly translucent and be soft to the touch of a knife in the centre.

Turn up the heat and pour in the balsamic vinegar so that the pan is deglazed and the fennel develops a caramelised effect on both sides. The vinegar will evaporate quite quickly but try not to let it all evaporate. Turn off the heat and leave to cool.

To serve, arrange 2 halves per person on a white plate. Drizzle the cooking juices around the fennel and season with freshly ground sea salt and pepper and some chopped chervil or fennel tops.

ABOVE: BRAISED FENNEL IN BALSAMIC VINEGAR
BELOW: TOMATO SALAD

TOMATO SALAD

SALADE DE TOMATES

This salad is only worth making with tomatoes ripened naturally in sunshine. Do not bother trying it with tomatoes that have been picked before they have been allowed to ripen fully; it will not taste the same. They should be firm but beautifully red, with all the goodness from the summer sun intact.

SERVES 4

8 MEDIUM TOMATOES OR 4 BEEFSTEAK TOMATOES,
WASHED
A BUNCH OF FRESH HERBS LIKE BASIL, TARRAGON,
CHERVIL OR CORIANDER, CHOPPED COARSELY
FRESHLY GROUND SEA SALT AND BLACK PEPPER TO
SEASON

FOR THE DRESSING

1 TABLESPOON FINE DIJON MUSTARD
1 TABLESPOON RED- OR WHITE-WINE VINEGAR
PINCH OF SALT
3 TABLESPOONS (APPROXIMATELY) SUNFLOWER OIL

Slice the tomatoes into rounds about 5 mm ($^1/_4$ inch) thick and arrange on a serving dish.

Put the mustard, vinegar and a pinch of salt in a small bowl or jar, and mix well. Add the sunflower oil slowly, stirring steadily with a fork rather as you would when making a mayonnaise, until the dressing has a smooth, even consistency.

Drizzle the dressing over the tomato rounds, sprinkle over the chopped herbs and some freshly ground black pepper and sea salt. Serve with fresh crusty bread.

SNAPPER WITH PRESERVED LEMONS

DAURADE AUX CITRONS CONFITS

This recipe could not be simpler — a fresh snapper, lemon and a sprinkling of herbs. It is ideal for the summer barbecue; instead of using a gratin dish, wrap the fish in foil and cook over vine-wood coals.

SERVES 4

1 LARGE OR 4 SMALL SNAPPER, CLEANED, GUTTED AND
SCALED
6–8 WEDGES OF PRESERVED LEMON
GROUND PEPPER AND SALT
2 TABLESPOONS LEMON JUICE
50 ml (2 fl oz) OLIVE OIL
1 TABLESPOON CRACKED CORIANDER SEEDS
FRESH CORIANDER TO GARNISH

In a shallow gratin dish (double thickness foil, if you are barbecuing) place 4 wedges of preserved lemon, sliced in two like a butterfly, so they sit flat in the dish. Place the fish on top of the lemon slices and grind sea salt and black pepper over the surface. Drizzle over the lemon juice and olive oil.

With a mortar and pestle, or food processor, crack the coriander seeds and scatter over the fish also. Finally add the rest of the preserved lemon, sliced again so that they do not sit too bulkily over the fish.

Bake in a hot oven, 230°C (450°F; gas mark 8), for 30 minutes, basting every now and then.

If barbecuing, the length of the cooking time will depend on the temperature of the coals, but allow 15–20 minutes. Garnish with freshly chopped coriander.

BARBECUES

GRILLADES

For the French, there is nothing left to chance, even with the simple barbecue. After all, the word comes from the French *barbe à la queue* meaning 'head to tail', a reference to the method of spit roasting a whole beast in olden times.

In this wine-growing area there is no shortage of the essential raw material, with its plentiful supply of vine wood. The locals would not dream of using a gas barbecue or buying charcoal.

Their charcoal is made from burning the vine wood prior to cooking the meat or fish, and even at this stage there is a choice of vine wood, each with its own properties which make it preferable for different kinds of barbecuing. The sarments, the long leaders which grow each year and which carry the grapes, are pruned off in the winter months, tied into faggots and stored in a dry place. They are the most highly perfumed, but the coals only last a short time, so they are used to grill things that only requires a few minutes' cooking.

The main trunks, which may be 30–100 years old, make excellent long-lasting coals. Though less perfumed, they are ideal for joints of meat or whole carcasses requiring 30–60 minutes' cooking. But the most highly prized are the elbows from which the sarments grow, which may be 2–5 years old. They are an ideal compromise; highly perfumed and reasonably long-lasting, they are sought after for cooking chops, steaks and magret de canard.

One of the secrets of successful barbecuing that we have discovered is to use a two-sided grill in which to hold the meat or fish securely. The grill has legs 5 cm (2 inches) long, which allows you to place it directly over the coals — no air gap, no air for the dripping fat to burn with, no flames, no more burnt offerings. It is simple and it works brilliantly.

In this region, the traditional Languedocien herbs — thyme, rosemary and bay — are used to flavour the barbecue. The herbs are either crumbled over the meat or fish, or are thrown onto the coals. The grill is then placed over the coals and the smoke and fumes of the burning herbs penetrate and perfume the food being grilled.

BARBECUED TUNA STEAKS

GRILLADE DE THON

When the Mediterranean blue-fin tuna is in season in early summer, we buy steaks 2–3 cm (1 inch) thick for barbecuing. When cooked, well charred on the outside and still pink and moist in the centre, it is as good as the best of beef steaks, if not better!

1 TUNA STEAK, 225 g (8 oz), PER PERSON
PEPPER AND SALT TO SEASON
SPRIGS THYME AND ROSEMARY
6–8 BAY LEAVES

Place the tuna steaks in a double-sided grill. Season with pepper and salt.

Throw the sprigs of thyme and rosemary and 3 or 4 bay leaves on to the barbecue coals, and immediately cover with the grill. Cook for 3–4 minutes.

Turn the grill over, throw more herbs on the coals, and cover with the grill again. Cook for a further 3–4 minutes, or until the outsides are well charred and the centre is still pink.

Serve straight away with boiled potatoes and a green salad.

BARBECUED PORK CHOPS

GRILLADE DE CÔTE DE PORC

The pork in France is of a very high standard and less expensive than beef or lamb. We have had to train our butcher to cut the chops thick, at least 2–3 cm (1 inch), otherwise they dry out too quickly. But thick-cut chops grilled over vine wood, with Languedocien herbs, are a meal fit for a king.

1 PORK CHOP, 225 g (8 oz), PER PERSON
SPRIGS THYME AND ROSEMARY
6–8 BAY LEAVES
FRESHLY GROUND PEPPER AND SALT

Place the chops in the double-sided grill. Crumble over half the thyme, rosemary and bay leaves. Season with pepper and salt. Place the grill over the barbecue coals, and cook rapidly for 4 minutes.

Turn the grill over, season again and crumble over the remaining herbs. Return the grill to the coals and cook for a further 4 minutes, until well charred on the outside, and cooked but still moist on the inside.

Serve with boiled potatoes and a green salad or Ratatouille (see page 58).

BARBECUED SARDINES

SARDINADE

1 kg (2 lb 4 oz) FRESH SARDINES OR SMALL SPRATS

When the sardines are in season in spring and summer they are readily available in the fish shops and markets. We buy a bagful and return home full of expectation. Laid out head to tail in two parallel rows on the grill, they look so inviting with their silvery bodies and bright black eyes. Once over the barbecue coals, their fats and juices drip onto the coals and produce an intense cloud of grey-white smoke which is so highly perfumed that your mouth cannot help watering in anticipation.

Wash the sardines or sprats and pat them dry with paper towels. Lay them out, head to tail, in 2 rows on the double-sided grill. Place the grill over the coals and cook for 2–3 minutes on each side, or until the outsides are crisp and the centres are still moist.

Serve with crusty bread and a well-chilled rosé wine. The flesh will come away easily from the backbone and head.

BARBECUED FATTENED-DUCK BREAST

GRILLADE DE MAGRET DE CANARD

Magret de canard is the breast from a duck which has been fattened on corn, for its liver to make foie gras. It is something of a delicacy in France, especially in the regions of Perigord and Gascony. An average breast weighs around 450 g (1 lb), which is more than ample for two people. It has an extremely delicious flavour, with the meat being dark red in colour, with a very dense consistency. One side of the breast has a thick layer of fat covering it, which is grilled over a very high heat so that the majority of the fat melts away, but keeps the meat beautifully moist. It is almost always served rare like a fine fillet of beef or charolais steak.

SERVES 2

1 MAGRET DE CANARD (DUCK BREAST), 450 g (1 lb)
COARSE-GROUND PEPPER AND SEA SALT
SPRIGS THYME AND ROSEMARY

With a sharp knife, score both sides of the magret with diagonal cuts about 5 mm ($^1/_4$ inch) deep, making a diamond pattern. Sprinkle coarse-grained sea salt on both sides.

Place the magret with the fat side down, so that it is cooked first, in the double-sided grill.

Throw sprigs of thyme and rosemary, and several bay leaves, onto the barbecue coals, and immediately cover with the grill. Cook for 4 minutes.

Turn over the grill. Throw on more herbs, and return the grill to the coals. Cook for a further 4 minutes, or until the meat is well charred on the outside but still pink, even bloody, on the inside. If you like your meat less pink, leave it to cook for 1–2 minutes longer, but do not overcook.

Remove the magret to a carving board and carve into slices 5 mm ($^1/_4$ inch) thick. Arrange on a serving dish and pour over the juices from carving the meat.

TOP: BARBECUED FATTENED-DUCK BREAST

BOTTOM: BAY IN FLOWER. BAY IS ONE OF THE THREE MAIN HERBS USED FOR BARBEQUES IN THE LANGUEDOC, ALONG WITH THYME AND ROSEMARY. IT IS POSSIBLE TO GATHER ALL THREE HERBS WHERE THEY GROW WILD ON THE GARRIGUES.

GRILLED EELS

ANGUILLES GRILLÉES À LA PERSILLADE

The first time we ate this dish was in a restaurant in Marennes near La Rochelle. We thought nothing would ever taste as good again. Now we have a local fisherman who brings us eels fresh from the river, from time to time, because he knows we like them so. They must be really fresh, of course, and not too large, not too small, and there has to be just the right amount of garlic, salt and parsley

SERVES 4

1 kg (2 lb 4 oz) FRESH EELS, GUTTED, SKINNED AND CLEANED
5 CLOVES OF GARLIC, CHOPPED FINELY
A LARGE BUNCH OF FLAT-LEAF PARSLEY, CHOPPED FINELY
SEA SALT TO SEASON
OLIVE OIL

Slice the eels down the centre, brush lightly with olive oil and sprinkle over plenty of chopped garlic, parsley and salt.

Grill over a vine-wood fire or under a very hot grill for 10–15 minutes, turning occasionally.

Serve hot with Pan-sautéed Potatoes (page 81).

RABBIT PROVENÇAL STYLE

LAPIN PROVENÇAL

Rabbit adapts well to most ingredients you put with it, coping with strong flavours as well as delicate. If you are able to get hold of a young wild rabbit, there is nothing more delicious than roasting it over a bed of coals. But it is equally delicious braised slowly in the oven on a bed of summer vegetables, with red wine.

SERVES 4

1 OVEN-READY RABBIT, APPROXIMATELY 1.4 kg (3 lb), JOINTED INTO 6 PIECES
2 MEDIUM AUBERGINES, SLICED
3 TABLESPOONS OLIVE OIL
1 LARGE ONION, COARSELY CHOPPED
6 MEDIUM TOMATOES, SKINNED AND CHOPPED
200 g (7 oz) BLACK OLIVES, STONED
A HANDFUL CHOPPED SAVORY
3 CLOVES GARLIC, FLATTENED UNDER THE BLADE OF A KNIFE
1 BAY LEAF
250 ml (8 fl oz) GOOD-QUALITY RED WINE
SALT AND PEPPER TO SEASON

Lay the slices of aubergine in a colander, sprinkle with sea salt and leave for 1 hour.

Warm the olive oil in a frying pan, and on a high heat brown the rabbit pieces on both sides. Remove with a slotted spoon and put on a paper towel to drain. Sauté the onion.

When the aubergine is ready, pat dry with paper towels. Pour the oil and the onion from the pan into a spacious casserole dish. Lay the slices of aubergine on top of them, then place the pieces of rabbit onto the aubergine. Sprinkle the chopped tomatoes, the olives and the savory over the top. Toss in the garlic and the bay leaf, then pour the wine evenly over the contents of the casserole, and season with salt and pepper. Place in a moderate oven, 180°C (350°F; gas mark 4), and cook for 1–1 1/2 hours, until the rabbit is tender. Serve very hot with a bowl of new potatoes with parsley butter.

PROVENÇAL ONION TART

PISSALADIÈRE

Said to be a speciality of the Nice region, this pizza-like tart is found sold in slices in most southern bakeries. It makes an ideal picnic snack or lunch-on-the-run, and an even better first course, served warm with a sharp green salad. It is usually made with a bread-dough base, which can often be a bit heavy for a first course, so we have adapted a traditional recipe, and substituted a lighter yeast pastry for the heavier. However, if you prefer, a plain shortcrust pastry will suffice.

Herbes de Provence is an aromatic mixture of thyme, rosemary, bay, basil and savory, usually dried, which is readily available pre-mixed in packets. It is most often added to flavour grilled meats and fish, vegetable dishes and savoury tarts.

SERVES 6

YEAST PASTRY

1 TEASPOON DRIED YEAST
150 ml (5 fl oz) WARM WATER
225 g (8 oz) WHITE FLOUR
1 TEASPOON SALT
2 TABLESPOONS OLIVE OIL

FOR THE FILLING

OLIVE OIL
650 g (1 lb 7 oz) SWEET ONIONS, SLICED FINELY
2 CLOVES GARLIC, CRUSHED
2 TOMATOES, SKINNED, SEEDED AND CHOPPED
FRESHLY GROUND SALT AND PEPPER
50 g (2 oz) ANCHOVY FILLETS
12 SMALL BLACK OLIVES, STONED
2 TEASPOONS HERBES DE PROVENCE OR FRESH THYME

Mix the yeast with the warm water and leave to stand for 5 minutes, until it starts to froth. Sieve the flour into a large glass bowl, mix in the salt, and make a well in the centre. When the yeast starter is ready, pour it into the flour, and add the olive oil. Mix well with the blade of a knife, and then start to knead with the heel of your hand. When the dough starts to come away from the sides of the bowl easily and feels nice and elastic, form a ball with the dough, cover it with a linen tea towel, and leave in a warm draught-free place for about an hour, until the dough has doubled in size.

Now heat some olive oil in a frying pan, and add the sliced onion and the garlic. Cover and cook gently until the onions are soft but still pale; do not let them burn or go brown. Add the chopped tomatoes and salt and pepper. Continue to cook until any liquid in the pan has reduced to almost nothing. Turn off the heat and leave the mixture to cool.

When the dough has risen, turn it out onto a floured surface and knead again for a minute or two, then make it into a ball again. Place this in the centre of a 30-cm (12-inch) baking tin. Using your knuckles and working quickly, carefully press the dough outward to the edges of the tin, until it completely covers the base and sides.

Tip the onion mixture into the centre, and spread it evenly so it is ideally half as thick again as the dough base. Make a criss-cross pattern over the top with the anchovies, then place the olives in the spaces. Sprinkle a little *Herbes de Provence* or fresh thyme over the top, and cover with a linen tea towel. Leave to rise for another 30 minutes in a warm, draught-free place. Bake in a very hot oven, 220°C (425°F; gas mark 7), for 25–30 minutes.

CHICKEN WITH LEMON
POULET AU CITRON

The strong lemon and thyme flavours in this dish create a refreshing combination. For a less French variation to this recipe omit the cream and serve with the cooking juices, with a sprinkling of freshly chopped chervil.

SERVES 4

1 MEDIUM-SIZED CHICKEN, CUT INTO PORTIONS
JUICE OF 2 LEMONS
GROUND BLACK PEPPER AND SALT
1/4–1/2 TEASPOON CAYENNE
4 TABLESPOONS OLIVE OIL
1 SMALL BUNCH FRESH THYME
125 ml (4 fl oz) CREAM

In a bowl, combine the lemon juice, some salt and pepper and the cayenne. Add the chicken pieces and marinate for a minimum of 1 hour — 3–4 hours if possible.

Drain the chicken pieces, retaining the marinade, and pat dry with a paper towel. In a cast-iron casserole, heat the olive oil and brown the chicken. Reduce the heat and sprinkle over the fresh thyme. Cover and leave to simmer gently for about 30 minutes.

Remove the chicken from the casserole and keep hot. Add the marinade to the juices in the casserole, along with the cream. Raise the heat and stir well, allowing the sauce to thicken, about 8 minutes. Adjust the seasoning if need be.

Lay the chicken in a warmed serving dish and pour over the sauce. Serve with new potatoes and a steaming bowl of fresh green beans.

BRAISED FARM CHICKEN WITH SAVORY
POULET FERMIER À LA SARRIETTE

The thing about chicken in France is that it really tastes like chicken. A large percentage of birds are raised free-range and fed on corn. Because of this, the meat is beautifully dense and tender, slightly yellow in colour as a result of the corn, and wonderfully flavoursome.

With this method of braising poultry the taste of the bird stands on its own, and there is little need to put much in the way of its delicious meat. A little wine perhaps and a handful of fresh herbs are all that is necessary in most cases. It is possible to buy battery-raised birds fed on meal, but we have been thoroughly seduced by the free-range chicken. So for this dish, whenever possible, choose a free-range, corn-fed bird.

SERVES 4

1–1.5 kg (2–3 lb) CHICKEN, CUT INTO PIECES
3–4 TABLESPOONS OLIVE OIL
1 LARGE ONION OR 2–3 SHALLOTS, FINELY CHOPPED
150 ml (5 fl oz) LIGHT DRY WHITE WINE
1 GENEROUS BUNCH SAVORY, COARSELY CHOPPED
GROUND BLACK PEPPER AND SALT

Heat the oven to 180°C (350°F; gas mark 4). Pat the chicken pieces dry with a paper towel.

In a heavy-based casserole, heat the olive oil over a high heat and place the chicken pieces in the oil. Brown the chicken quickly then set aside.

Still with the casserole on a high heat, sweat the onions until they are opaque — about 2–3 minutes. Add the white wine to deglaze the juices in the pan, and reduce the heat to low. Place the chicken back in the juices, sprinkle over the chopped savory and season with salt and pepper. Cover the casserole and place in the oven for about 40 minutes, or until the chicken is tender.

Serve with the cooking juices and an assortment of steamed buttered spring vegetables.

RAGOUT OF GUINEA FOWL

RAGOÛT DE PINTADEAU

The guinea fowl is an unusual-looking bird with black and white speckled plumage. The flesh is yellowish in colour and it has a delicate gamey flavour. These days it is commercially reared both free-range and in batteries, and is readily available in French butcher's shops, supermarkets and in local markets. It can be prepared in any way suitable for pheasant or chicken, and while the younger birds are superb for roasting, preferably on a high heat, quickly, so they do not dry out, an adult bird is perhaps a better choice for this dish, cooked slowly in its own juices with fresh herbs.

SERVES 4

1 MEDIUM-SIZED GUINEA FOWL, JOINTED
SALT AND PEPPER TO SEASON
2–3 TABLESPOONS OLIVE OIL
1 LARGE SWEET ONION, DICED
2 CLOVES GARLIC, CRUSHED UNDER THE BLADE OF A
KNIFE
1 BUNCH FRESH LEMON THYME
150 ml (5 fl oz) DRY WHITE WINE OR ROSÉ
FRESH THYME LEAVES, TO GARNISH

Season the guinea fowl with salt and pepper. Heat the oil in a cast-iron casserole dish, and lightly brown the pieces of guinea fowl on a high heat. Remove from the casserole with a slotted spoon, and place on a plate to one side for the moment.

Sauté the onion and garlic in the same oil for about 5–8 minutes on a medium heat. Add the lemon thyme, raise the heat and place the guinea fowl on top. Add the wine to the hot casserole and simmer for a few minutes. Cover and place in a moderate oven, 180°C (350°F; gas mark 4) for 40–50 minutes.

Transfer the guinea fowl to a hot serving dish, spoon over the onions, herbs and pan juices, and decorate with some fresh sprigs of thyme.

QUAIL WITH CRÈME FRAÎCHE AND GRAPES

CAILLES À LA CRÈME FRAÎCHE ET AUX RAISINS

A light, summery dish with fresh tangy flavours. Perfect for a summer's evening, and best enjoyed outside with good companions and plenty of dry white wine.

SERVES 4

4 QUAIL, HEADS REMOVED
SALT AND PEPPER
4 SMALL CLOVES GARLIC, PEELED
4 GOOD-SIZED SPRIGS THYME
2–3 TABLESPOONS OLIVE OIL OR UNSALTED BUTTER
3 SHALLOTS, CHOPPED
OR
1 LARGE ONION, CHOPPED
1 BAY LEAF
100 ml (3 fl oz) WHITE WINE
1 CUP SWEET BLACK GRAPES, CUT IN HALF LENGTHWAYS
100 g (3 oz) CRÈME FRAÎCHE
A FEW SPRIGS OF FRESH THYME TO GARNISH

Season the quail with salt and pepper, and into the cavity of each bird place a clove of garlic and a sprig of thyme. Make a small incision in the skin at the base of the breast and cavity opening. Carefully tuck the legs into the incision and tuck the wings into the sides of the legs.

Heat the oil or butter in a casserole, and sauté the shallots on a medium heat. Remove and put to one side.

Raise the heat and brown the quail. Return the shallots to the casserole, add the bay leaf and the white wine. Wait until the wine has come to the boil and reduced a little, then cover and put into a moderate oven, 180°C (350°F; gas mark 4), for 15–20 minutes. The quail should be slightly pink inside and nicely moist.

When cooked, remove from the casserole, place in a serving dish and keep warm.

Add the grapes to the juices and cook for a few minutes. Add the crème fraîche on a low heat and stir well. Pour over the quail and garnish with fresh thyme.

SPAGHETTI WITH PUTANESCA SAUCE

SPAGHETTI À LA PUTANESCA

As an alternative to meat and fish dishes, this pasta dish provides a complete contrast, with its strong, robust piquancy. The folklore surrounding its origins suggests that it was a favourite with the prostitutes of Naples.

SERVES 4

300 g (10 oz) SPAGHETTI, FRESH OR DRIED
2–3 TABLESPOONS OLIVE OIL
6 CLOVES GARLIC, CRUSHED
500 g (1 lb 2 oz) TOMATO PURÉE
18 BLACK OLIVES, STONED AND ROUGHLY CHOPPED
1 TABLESPOON CAPERS, FINELY CHOPPED
1 TEASPOON FRESH OREGANO, FINELY CHOPPED
PINCH OF CHILLI POWDER (OPTIONAL)
GROUND BLACK PEPPER AND SALT TO TASTE
4–5 ANCHOVY FILLETS

Heat the olive oil in a cast-iron frying pan or casserole. When the oil is medium hot, add the garlic and cook until it is just starting to brown.

Add the tomato purée, olives, capers, oregano, chilli powder, ground black pepper and salt. Stir well. Cover and allow to simmer for 15–20 minutes.

Remove the lid and continue to simmer for another 15 minutes, allowing the sauce to thicken and reduce a little. Stir occasionally.

Five minutes before serving, add the anchovies and stir.

Bring water, with a little olive oil, to the boil in a pan and add the spaghetti. Cook until al dente, stirring frequently. Strain and serve, with the sauce poured over.

SPAGHETTI WITH TOMATO AND GARLIC

SPAGHETTI AUX TOMATES ET À L'AIL

This is one of those wonderful summer dishes, bursting with taste, quick to prepare, to be enjoyed in the sunshine.

SERVES 4–6

500 g (1 lb 2 oz) SPAGHETTI, FRESH OR DRIED
4–6 SUN-RIPENED TOMATOES, SKINNED AND DICED
2–3 CLOVES GARLIC, CRUSHED
1–2 TEASPOONS CHOPPED FRESH OREGANO
4 TABLESPOONS OLIVE OIL
BLACK PEPPER AND SEA SALT, COARSELY GROUND
CHOPPED PARSLEY TO GARNISH

Heat water in a saucepan until boiling. Add the spaghetti and cook, stirring frequently, until al dente. Strain and allow to cool.

In a large bowl, mix together the tomatoes, garlic, oregano and olive oil. Season with the black pepper and salt.

When the spaghetti has cooled, add it to the tomatoes, herbs and olive oil. Toss well and serve with a garnish of chopped parsley.

ROASTED POTATOES WITH AUBERGINE

POMMES DE TERRE ET AUBERGINES RÔTIES

When you tire of plain roasted potatoes, though it is difficult given the varieties of potato available, this mixture makes a nice change, and goes well with roasted and grilled meats.

SERVES 4

1 LARGE AUBERGINE, THICKLY SLICED THEN QUARTERED
500 g (1 lb 2 oz) FLOURY ROASTING POTATOES, PEELED AND HALVED
2 STALKS FRESH ROSEMARY
FRESHLY GROUND SEA SALT AND BLACK PEPPER
3–4 TABLESPOONS OLIVE OIL, DUCK OR GOOSE FAT

Place the aubergine in a colander and sprinkle salt over. Cover with a plate and leave to drain for 1 hour. Wipe dry with paper towels.

Parboil the potatoes for 10–15 minutes, then drain.

Tip the potatoes into an ovenproof dish and arrange the pieces of aubergine among them. Sprinkle over the rosemary leaves, salt and pepper, then drizzle the olive oil evenly over the surface. Roast in a moderately hot oven, 190°C (375°F; gas mark 5), for 30–40 minutes, basting now and again, until the potatoes and aubergine are nicely cooked on the inside and crisp on the outside.

SWEET AND SOUR AUBERGINES

AUBERGINES AIGRE-DOUCE

While the aubergine is an important part of Languedocien cooking, this recipe, with its subtle contrasts of sweet and sour, owes its origins to India. It makes a very tasty entrée or side dish to grilled meats or curry.

SERVES 4

900 g (2 lb) AUBERGINES
VEGETABLE OIL
1 TEASPOON PANCHPHORAN (SEE BELOW)
1 LARGE ONION, SLICED
2–3 TEASPOONS RAW SUGAR
2 TEASPOONS LEMON JUICE
PINCH OF CHILLI POWDER
1 TEASPOON SESAME SEEDS, ROASTED

Cut the aubergines roughly into 1–2.5 cm ($^1/_2$–1 inch) cubes and put them in a sieve or colander. Sprinkle with salt and set aside to drain for 30–60 minutes. Pat dry with a kitchen towel.

Pour 1 cm ($^1/_2$ inch) of oil into a wok or large frying pan and bring to a medium heat. Add the aubergine in a single layer and cook until it starts to brown, turning so all sides are cooked. You may need to do this operation in several stages because of the bulk of the aubergine. Add oil as needed. Set the aubergine aside.

Make the panchphoran by mixing a pinch of each of the following: whole seeds of black mustard, cumin, fennel, fenugreek, and kalonji (nigella or onion seed). If you cannot find the kalonji, leave it out.

Add 2–3 tablespoons of oil to the wok or frying pan, and bring to a medium heat. Throw in the panchphoran and cook for a few seconds until it starts to pop. Add the onion and sauté until it starts to brown.

Add the aubergine, sugar, lemon juice, chilli and sesame seeds. Stir while cooking for 1–2 minutes. Serve warm or cold.

GRATINÉED AUBERGINE LANGUEDOCIEN STYLE

AUBERGINES AU GRATIN LANGUEDOCIEN

A dish to eat on its own with a crusty baguette, as a light lunch, or to accompany roasted or barbecued meats and fish.

SERVES 4

2 AUBERGINES, SLICED THICKLY
4–6 TOMATOES, CUT INTO HALVES
50 ml (2 fl oz) OLIVE OIL FOR SAUTÉEING THE AUBERGINE
AND TOMATOES
75–100 g (3–4 oz) BREADCRUMBS
SALT AND PEPPER
2 TABLESPOONS CHOPPED PARSLEY
2 CLOVES GARLIC, CHOPPED
2 TABLESPOONS OLIVE OIL

Place the aubergine in a colander, sprinkle with salt, and leave to drain for 1 hour. Pat dry with paper towels.

In a frying pan, lightly sauté the tomato halves in a little oil. Place on a dish to one side for the moment. Add more oil to the pan, and sauté the aubergine until it is brown on both sides. You will need to add more oil from time to time, as the aubergines soak it up. Drain on a paper towel.

Arrange the aubergine and tomato in alternate layers in a gratin dish, sprinkle generously with breadcrumbs, season with salt and pepper, and add the chopped parsley and garlic. Drizzle olive oil over the top, and brown in the oven or under the grill.

RED PEPPER AND ONION CONFITURE

CONFITURE AUX OIGNONS ET AUX POIVRONS ROUGES

A superb companion to summertime grilled meats and fish. The flavours meld together beautifully and add a colourful splash, with lots of nutty sauce for mopping up with a chunk of crusty wholemeal bread. If you like a bit of heat in your food, add half a dried and seeded chilli. (If you are not fond of capsicums, replace them with roasted tomatoes.)

4 TABLESPOONS OLIVE OIL
3 LARGE, SWEET ONIONS, HALVED AND SLICED LENGTHWAYS
2 LARGE CLOVES GARLIC, PEELED AND FLATTENED UNDER A KNIFE BLADE
2–3 RIPE RED CAPSICUMS, SLICED LENGTHWAYS
2 TABLESPOONS BROWN SUGAR
SALT AND PEPPER TO SEASON

Heat the oil in a roomy, heavy-based frying pan or casserole, add the onions and garlic, and sweat them slowly over a medium heat. After about 5 minutes, add the capsicums and sprinkle the sugar over the top. Stir well and cover with a lid. Continue to cook slowly in this fashion, stirring every now and then, for 20–25 minutes, until the confiture is nicely blended, soft and slightly caramelised.

Serve hot or cold.

COURGETTES IN BLACK BUTTER

COURGETTES AU BEURRE NOIR

This is a great way of preparing courgettes either as a light entrée or as an accompaniment to meat dishes. It is equally good with fennel, celery, asparagus and cardoon, which is a southern European vegetable related to the artichoke plant, whose stalks are eaten as a vegetable here in late autumn and early winter. The sage can also be replaced with parsley.

SERVES 4

6 SMALL TO MEDIUM COURGETTES
50 g (2 oz) BUTTER
6 GENEROUS SPRIGS FRESH SAGE
3 TABLESPOONS FRESHLY GRATED PARMESAN CHEESE
FRESHLY GROUND SEA SALT AND BLACK PEPPER

Cook the courgettes whole in salted boiling water until they are tender but not mushy. Drain in a colander, and trim the ends. Slice the courgettes diagonally into pieces, and place them in a serving dish.

In a small saucepan, melt the butter with the sage leaves and cook until the butter has turned dark brown. Sprinkle the parmesan over the courgettes, season with salt and pepper, and pour over the butter and sage. Serve immediately.

VEGETABLE RAGOUT
RATATOUILLE

A traditional ratatouille will always have the same basic ingredients; onions, aubergines, sweet peppers, tomatoes and courgettes. The quantities and optional extras like garlic and fresh herbs will vary, but the cooking oil must always be olive oil. The puritans demand that each vegetable must be cooked separately first, then combined and cooked until they reach a creamy consistency. Others have less rigid ideas. Our personal preference is to leave out the courgettes, cook the onions and aubergines separately, then combine the rest. The perfect subject for a good meal-time debate, a pastime the French are greatly fond of. Without doubt, however, it is generally agreed that this delicious concoction goes brilliantly with virtually all roasted, braised and grilled meats. It even works well with omelettes and scrambled eggs, and is superb just on its own.

SERVES 4

2 LARGE AUBERGINES, SLICED INTO THICK ROUNDS, THEN QUARTERED
100 ml (3 fl oz) FRUITY OLIVE OIL
2 MEDIUM-SIZED SWEET ONIONS, PEELED AND CHOPPED COARSELY
3 LARGE CLOVES GARLIC, FLATTENED UNDER THE BLADE OF A KNIFE
4 LARGE TOMATOES, SKINNED AND CHOPPED, OR A CAN OF WHOLE TOMATOES IN THEIR JUICE
3 SWEET PEPPERS, TRIMMED OF STALKS, SEEDED AND CUT INTO STRIPS
THYME OR BASIL, OR A LITTLE CHILLI (OPTIONAL)
FRESHLY GROUND SEA SALT AND BLACK PEPPER
COARSELY CHOPPED FLAT-LEAF PARSLEY, TO GARNISH

Place the aubergines in a colander, sprinkle with salt, and cover with a plate. Leave for 1 hour to express any excess water. After an hour, drain well and pat dry with paper towels.

Heat a little of the olive oil in a large, heavy-based casserole or frying pan. Throw in the onions and garlic, and cook on a medium heat, until they are soft but not brown. Remove to a side plate with a slotted spoon. Add some more oil and cook the aubergine. They will soak up a lot of the oil so you may need to add more as they cook. Allow the aubergine to brown very slightly, stirring every few minutes. Pour the onions, garlic and their juices back into the casserole, add the tomatoes, peppers and any herbs you wish. Stir well, reduce the heat to a slow simmer, cover and leave to cook until the vegetables have cooked well and reached your preferred consistency. We like our ratatouille to be good and sloppy, without being watery. Serve hot or cold, with plenty of fresh bread to mop up the juices.

NOTE: If adding courgettes, put them in after you have cooked the aubergine.

GREEN BEANS WITH GARLIC
HARICOTS VERTS À LA PERSILLADE

A great way to eat green beans in the summertime and a perfect marriage with barbecued and grilled meats, although a plate of these is delicious enough on its own.

SERVES 4

500 g (1 lb 2 oz) GREEN BEANS, TOPPED AND TAILED
2–3 TABLESPOONS OLIVE OIL
1–2 CLOVES GARLIC, PEELED
A GENEROUS HANDFUL CHOPPED PARSLEY
FRESHLY GROUND BLACK PEPPER AND SEA SALT

Wash the beans and steam them lightly for about 5 minutes. Drain straight away, then run them under cold water to retain a good colour.

In a frying pan, heat the olive oil and add the beans. Chop the parsley with the garlic and toss over the beans.

Continue cooking the beans over a medium heat for another 5–8 minutes, until they are cooked but still al dente. Turn out into an earthenware bowl and garnish liberally with pepper and sea salt. Eat while piping hot.

GOAT CHEESE WITH EAU-DE-VIE

FROMAGE À L'EAU-DE-VIE

A traditional way of using up leftover goat cheese. This quantity will last well as the flavour is quite potent, but delicious all the same, so you only need a small amount to satisfy. It must be made in an earthenware jar that can be sealed with a lid. And *les anciens* suggest that it is always best to mix a little of the previous mixture with the new to give it that little *je ne sais quoi*. It is also very tasty made with a strong blue cheese like Roquefort, but whichever you choose, use approximately 3 parts cheese to 2 parts fromage frais.

1 MATURED GOAT CHEESE, APPROXIMATELY 80 g (3 oz)
1 FRESH GOAT CHEESE, APPROXIMATELY 80 g (3 oz)
125 g (4 oz) FROMAGE FRAIS
1 CLOVE GARLIC, PEELED AND CRUSHED
1 GOOD SPRIG THYME OR SAVORY, FINELY CHOPPED
1 TEASPOON EAU-DE-VIE
1 TEASPOON FRUITY OLIVE OIL
FRESHLY GROUND SEA SALT AND PEPPER, TO TASTE

Crumble the mature goat cheese into a bowl, and blend in the fresh goat cheese and fromage frais with a fork.

Add the garlic and thyme, and mix well. Now add the eau-de vie alternately with the olive oil, little by little, until the mixture resembles thick cream. Taste and adjust the seasoning to your preference.

Spoon the mixture into an earthenware jar, and smooth out the surface. Seal the jar carefully, and store in a cool place for at least 1 or 2 weeks before using.

Serve with nutty rye bread and fresh pears or figs. This mixture will keep for approximately 2 months.

For the blue cheese version, leave out the garlic and thyme.

POACHED VINEYARD PEACHES
PÊCHES DE VIGNE POCHÉES

In the wine-growing regions of the Midi they cultivate a variety of peach which is to die for. We simply call it the vineyard peach, but to the locals it is known as *Les Tétons de Vénus*. It belongs to the white peach family, has a highly coloured skin with deep blush-pink flesh, and its fragrance is intoxicating. Sadly, it has a very short season, ripening around mid- to late August. So for a few precious weeks we obtain as many as we can, usually from certain producers in our local market, or friends in the village who will generously spare some, and treat our guests' tastebuds to a hedonist's sensation. Even if you cannot locate highly perfumed vineyard peaches, a simple yellow peach will excel in this syrup.

SERVES 4

4 RIPE PEACHES, WASHED AND DRIED
250 ml (8 fl oz) WATER
250 g (9 oz) WHITE SUGAR
1 MADAGASCAR VANILLA POD, SPLIT IN HALF
JUICE OF A LEMON
1 FRESH BAY LEAF
4 STAR ANISE
150 ml (5 fl oz) MUSCAT

Combine the water and sugar in a large saucepan and bring to the boil, stirring as you go, so that all the sugar dissolves. Add the vanilla pod, lemon juice, bay, star anise and 100 ml (4 fl oz) muscat. Add the peaches and adjust the heat so that the liquid is gently simmering. The length of cooking time will depend on the size of the peaches, but generally 20 minutes will be ample.

Carefully lift the peaches out of the syrup with a slotted spoon, and put to one side to cool. Continue to reduce the syrup, raising the heat, until the liquid has reduced by two-thirds. Stir in the last 50 ml (2 fl oz) of muscat, pass through a sieve and leave to cool.

When the peaches are cool remove the skins; they will come away very easily. Carefully slice the peaches in half and remove the stone, or alternatively they can be left whole. Place 2 peach halves or 1 whole peach on 4 separate serving plates, and pour over the syrup. Garnish with fresh mint leaves or borage flowers if desired, and serve with a small glass of lightly chilled muscat.

PEACH SOUP
SOUPE AUX PÊCHES

The search is always on during the baking summer months for cooling, light desserts that do not leave you with the feeling that you are going to be spending the rest of the night wrestling with the bed sheets and your digestive system. This simple combination of tangy white peaches and refreshing green mint makes an agreeable finale to any light summer menu.

SERVES 4

6 RIPE WHITE PEACHES
500–700 ml (16–24 fl oz) WATER
50 ml (2 fl oz) PASTIS (SEE PAGE 86)
1 VANILLA BEAN, SPLIT
3 STAR ANISE
200 g (6 oz) SUGAR
1–2 TABLESPOONS FRESH GREEN MINT, CHOPPED

Place the water, pastis, vanilla bean and star anise in a large saucepan. Stir in the sugar until it dissolves. Heat the syrup until it boils then reduce the heat to a simmer and add the peaches. Place a saucer right-side up on top of the peaches, so that they stay under the syrup. Cook for 5–8 minutes, no longer. Drain the peaches and leave to cool.

When cool, remove the skins and stones, and slice the peaches roughly into a glass dish, taking care to keep any of the peach juice that escapes as you do this. Add it to the peaches. Stir in the chopped mint, spoon into individual glass dishes, and serve with a lightly chilled glass of dessert wine.

BLACKCURRANT SORBET

SORBET AUX CASSIS

This cassis sorbet is always made with fresh, home-grown blackcurrants which some very generous English friends of ours donate at the beginning of each summer.

It is not necessary to use an ice-cream maker to make sorbet but it does help. If you do not have one, make the sorbet well in advance so that the mixture has time to freeze — at least 6 hours.

SERVES 6–8

250 g (9 oz) CASTOR SUGAR
500 ml (16 fl oz) WATER
400 g (14 oz) BLACKCURRANTS, WASHED, TOPPED AND TAILED
JUICE OF 1/2 LEMON
1 EGG WHITE
FRESH MINT TO GARNISH

Prepare the syrup by dissolving the castor sugar in the water in a large saucepan. Add the blackcurrants and the lemon juice. Bring to the boil then allow the liquid to cool.

Purée the mixture in a food processor or blender. Put the purée into an ice-cream maker and leave to work for about an hour. When the mixture begins to freeze pour into a container and place in the freezer until required.

If you do not have an ice-cream maker, pour the mixture into a container and place in the freezer for at least 5–6 hours. Every 2 hours check the mixture by running a fork through it, until it is frozen.

Half an hour before serving remove the sorbet from the freezer and leave it to soften slightly. Five minutes before you serve the sorbet, tip the contents into the food processor, add the white of an egg and process quickly until the texture is light and fluffy.

Serve in chilled parfait glasses with some fresh mint leaves.

TOMATO SORBET

SORBET À LA TOMATE

Another tomato recipe that is best made with summer sun-ripened tomatoes. Artificially ripened substitutes just will not produce enough flavour. This sorbet makes a superbly light beginning or end to a summer meal, and can easily be made a day or two in advance.

SERVES 4–6

4 VERY LARGE, RIPE TOMATOES, SKINNED
2 DROPS TABASCO OR CHILLI SAUCE
JUICE OF 1/2 LEMON
SEA SALT AND FRESHLY GROUND BLACK PEPPER TO TASTE
1 EGG WHITE
FRESH BASIL, CHERVIL OR TARRAGON SPRIGS

Cut the tomatoes in half and squeeze the seeds out over a sieve, so that you retain the juice but can easily dispose of the seeds.

Chop the tomatoes and place them in a food processor or blender along with the reserved juices, tabasco or chilli sauce, lemon juice, salt and pepper. Purée until the mixture is smooth, pour into a shallow freezer container and leave to freeze until it is a mushy consistency — about 3 hours.

When the sorbet has reached the right consistency, give it another quick whiz in the food processor or blender. Beat the egg white until it forms stiff peaks, and gently fold it into the sorbet thoroughly. Return the mixture to the freezer container, and continue freezing until it is firm. This will take longer because of the beaten egg whites, so allow 2–3 hours.

Spoon into chilled wine glasses, top with a sprig of fresh tarragon, basil or chervil and serve immediately.

BAKED FIGS

FIGUES CUITES AU FOUR

SERVES 4

12 RIPE FIGS, WASHED AND DRIED
50 g (2 oz) MUSCOVADO SUGAR
2 TABLESPOONS WATER OR LIQUEUR OF YOUR CHOICE

In late August the fig trees around our little village are heavy with ripening fruit. With such an abundance of grapes and stone fruit in the valley over spring and summer, the birds are already so fat and full of what has gone before that their interest in the succulent flesh of the figs is minimal. All the better for us! I can go out on my bicycle along the river road almost every day and fill my basket with more than we need to spoil our guests, to make jam, or for bottling. Our neighbour has a large white fig tree which bears the most beautifully perfumed figs, my favourites for this ridiculously simple dish. For stalwart fig lovers, one mouthful and you will think you have died and gone to heaven.

Heat the oven to 180°C (350°F; gas mark 4). Place all the figs in an ovenproof baking dish and sprinkle the muscovado sugar over the top of them. Then sprinkle the water or liqueur over the figs and sugar.

Place the dish in the oven and cook for 20–40 minutes, or until the figs are soft and the juice and sugar have melded together to make a syrupy sauce. It is a good idea to baste the fruit from time to time while they are cooking.

Remove from the oven when cooked and allow to cool. Serve at room temperature, or chilled, with the syrup spooned over the fruit and a little crème fraîche.

FIG TORTE

TOURTE AUX FIGUES

This recipe is like a pavlova, but with figs mixed into the meringue. Ideally, fresh red or purple figs are preferable, but if you cannot get them try soaking dried figs overnight in a little apple juice, a sweet wine like muscat or liqueur. The important thing is that the figs should be mashable, not firm.

SERVES 4

250 g (9 oz) FRESH FIGS, PEELED AND MASHED
OR
250 g (9 oz) DRIED FIGS, SOAKED OVERNIGHT, THEN
DRAINED AND MASHED
4 EGG WHITES
PINCH OF SALT
225 g (8 oz) CASTOR SUGAR
4 TEASPOONS CORNFLOUR
2 TEASPOONS VINEGAR
1/2 TEASPOON VANILLA ESSENCE

Preferably in a copper bowl, beat the egg whites with the pinch of salt until very stiff. You may prefer to do this with an electric mixer.

Add the castor sugar carefully, one spoonful at a time. The mixture will go even stiffer when beaten again. Add the cornflour, vinegar and vanilla essence, and beat them into the mixture. Fold in the figs quickly, and turn the mixture into a greased, shallow, ovenproof dish. Hollow out the centre slightly.

Bake in a preheated oven, 140°C (275°F; gas mark 1), for 75–90 minutes. Remove from the oven when cooked, and allow to cool. Like a pavlova, the torte will flatten as it cools but remain nicely chewy inside. Serve with crème fraîche and a glass of slightly chilled muscat.

VERVAIN SORBET

SORBET À LA VERVEINE

In early spring the lemon verbena tree in our front garden starts to shoot with tiny young green leaves. By June it is a mass of verdant green with delicate white flowers. In the early mornings, as I brush past it on my way to collect the day's fresh bread and croissants, the pungent scent of fresh lemon wafts up to meet me. It is this scent that is captured in the taste of a tisane made from an infusion of the leaves, said to be very good for one's well-being — or in this soothing sorbet — a refreshing ending to a satisfying meal at the height of summer.

SERVES 4

225 g (8 oz) CASTOR SUGAR
425 ml (12 fl oz) WATER
A LARGE HANDFUL FRESH LEMON VERBENA LEAVES
2 EGG WHITES
SOME SPRIGS OF THE TIPS OF LEMON VERBENA
A HANDFUL OF BORAGE FLOWERS, IF YOU HAVE THEM

Dissolve the sugar in the water and bring it to the boil. Simmer until all the sugar is dissolved then take the syrup off the heat and cool for a few minutes.

Chop the lemon verbena leaves roughly and place in a glass bowl. Pour over the hot syrup and put to one side to infuse until cold.

Strain the syrup off the leaves and pour into a container. Freeze for 2–3 hours, until the mixture is mushy. In a food processor or blender, whisk the egg whites into the half-frozen syrup and refreeze.

Remove the sorbet from the freezer at least 3 minutes before serving. Grate the sorbet with a fork or process in the blender again. Spoon the sorbet quickly into chilled parfait glasses and decorate with lemon verbena leaves and borage flowers. This sorbet also makes a pleasant 'palate cleanser' between courses.

LAVENDER SORBET

SORBET À LA LAVANDE

There are few sights in a southern French summer quite as awe-inspiring as lavender-covered hills in full bloom. The other sight that makes my heart flutter with pleasure almost as much is in the month of March, when the wisteria that covers our sunny terrace is in full, heavenly scented bloom. Sadly, wisteria blooms are very fragile and do not take kindly to cooking, but lavender does, and with a little help from some sweet muscat wine, makes this deliciously soothing sorbet. For this recipe and Lavender Sugar (see opposite) use highly perfumed French lavender flowers.

SERVES 4

185 ml (6 fl oz) MUSCAT
55 g (2 oz) FRESH FRENCH LAVENDER FLOWERS
150 ml (1/4 PINT) WATER
200 g (7 oz) LAVENDER SUGAR, SIEVED
JUICE OF A LEMON
3 EGG WHITES, BEATEN STIFF

In a glass or enamel saucepan, heat the muscat slowly to just warm. Remove from the heat, add the lavender flowers and set aside for 10 minutes to infuse, as you would a herbal tea.

Strain the liquid through a sieve and squeeze out as much of the liquid left in the lavender flowers as you can. Add the water and stir in the lavender sugar until dissolved. Add the lemon juice.

Beat the egg whites with a pinch of salt until they form stiff peaks, then fold them gently into the syrup.

Pour into an ice-cream maker or a container and freeze; allow about 4–5 hours for the mixture to freeze. When the sorbet begins to freeze, turn the mixture into the food processor and process for a minute or two. Turn out into a container and freeze until required.

LAVENDER SUGAR

SUCRE PARFUMÉ À LA LAVANDE

225 g (8 oz) CASTOR SUGAR
A SMALL BUNCH FRESH LAVENDER FLOWERS, STALKS REMOVED

In an airtight jar, layer the lavender flowers with the castor sugar until the jar is full. Leave in a warm, sunny spot for a day, and then store. Sieve the sugar before using.

APRICOT JAM

CONFITURE D'ABRICOTS

Another favourite with our guests at breakfast time — this has to be one of the best of all jams for spooning over a warm, buttery croissant.

3 kg (6 lb 12 oz) FRESH RIPE APRICOTS, WASHED, HALVED AND STONED
475 ml (14 fl oz) WATER
1–4 APRICOT KERNELS, BLANCHED
3 kg (6 lb 12 oz) SUGAR

Put the apricots into the jamming pan with the water, and gently cook until the fruit is soft and pulpy. Blanch the kernels in a small amount of water and add them to the pulp.

Add the sugar to the pulp, stirring as you go, and raise the heat to a rolling boil as quickly as possible. Test and when the right setting consistency is achieved, pot in warm, sterilised jars and seal.

RED PEPPERS PRESERVED IN OLIVE OIL WITH GARLIC

POIVRONS ROUGES CONFITS

Sweet red peppers make a great addition to many summer dishes, as well as a tangy pesto. We keep a jar of preserved peppers in the refrigerator to dip into when the need arises. There is no short cut to the laborious job of roasting and peeling the peppers beforehand, but it is worth the effort just the same. The left-over oil can be used for cooking, or flavouring salad dressings.

6–8 LARGE SWEET RED CAPSICUMS, WASHED AND DRIED
2 CLOVES GARLIC, PEELED
250–300 ml (8–10 fl oz) FIRST-PRESSING OLIVE OIL

Cut the peppers in half, trim off the stalks, and scrape out the seeds. Chargrill the peppers either under a hot grill or over a gas flame. As soon as the peppers are well blistered and charred, place them in an airtight plastic bag, and leave for 5–10 minutes. When the peppers have cooled a little, rub off the charred skins and trim off any bits that are too burnt.

Place the skinned peppers in a sterilised glass jar, add the cloves of garlic, and pour in enough olive oil to cover the peppers. Seal and store in the refrigerator.

SUN-DRIED TOMATOES

TOMATES SECHÉES AU SOLEIL

While we were on holiday in Nice, we visited the famous Friday market at Ventemiglia, a short train ride over the Franco/Italian border. There I found a jolly, plump-cheeked Italian man selling kilos of sun-dried tomatoes and red peppers. No fancy glass jars with special wrappings, just literally loose mountains of them to choose from. I bought several kilos of each, and returned home to bottle them in oil myself.

If you find you have an excess of tomatoes in your summer garden, or you find imported sun-dried tomatoes too expensive, it takes little time and a small amount of patience to prepare them for yourself. The most important thing is to make sure that the olive oil is of good quality, and you also need a good dry, sunny place to prepare them. If the climate you live in is humid, it is better to try drying the tomatoes in a very low-temperature oven. They make a great tangy pesto as well as a flavoursome base in casseroles. This recipe will make enough to fill two 1-litre glass preserving jars. Red or yellow peppers can be dried in the same way.

5 kg (11 lb) RIPE, GOOD-QUALITY TOMATOES
50 g (2 oz) COARSE-GRAINED OR GROUND SEA SALT
10 BASIL LEAVES (OPTIONAL)
1 LITRE (2 PINTS) EXTRA VIRGIN OLIVE OIL

Wash the tomatoes well and cut them in half. Scoop out the seeds with a teaspoon.

Cover 2 large wire cooling racks with absorbent kitchen towels, and lay the tomatoes face down to drain.

After 15 minutes turn them up the right way, and sprinkle lightly with salt. Remove the soiled kitchen towels, and turn the tomato halves upside down again on the racks, close together.

If you are sun-drying the tomatoes, place them in a sunny, dry, elevated position, so that the warm air can pass all around them. We put ours on our terrace, with the racks propped between the backs of two chairs. Providing the day is good and hot, around 26–27°C, a full day's sun should be sufficient to dry them. If they require more sun, put them out for a second day.

If you are oven-drying the tomatoes, a temperature of 70–80°C (175°F) is ample to dry the fruit overnight. It is important to allow the air to circulate, so prop open the oven door with the handle of a wooden spoon.

When the tomatoes have dried, they should still be slightly fleshy and a brownish/orange/red colour. Place them in 2 sterilised 1-litre glass jars, and add some basil leaves if you wish. Pour over the olive oil, until it completely covers the tomatoes. Seal and store on a dark, cool shelf.

AUTUMN

LANGUEDOCIEN MARINATED OLIVES

OLIVES PARFUMÉES AUX HERBES LANGUEDOCIENNES

In most French market places on market day, you will find at least one vendor selling olives — but not just one or two varieties. In some cases he will have between 12 and 20 different types, from the simple fruity Lucques green olives of the Languedoc in their own brine, to Picholine (from the Gard region), à la grecque (black kalamatas in oil), Provençal (black in olive oil with Herbes de Provence), Spanish-style éscabèche (green prepared with chilli, vinegar and spices), aux anchois (green stuffed with anchovies) and so on, all beautifully displayed in great glistening mounds. As well as his impressive array of olives, he will sell capers in brine, cured anchovies, salted cod for making brandade, marinated fava beans and spices arranged in little cellophane packets, all carefully labelled. And at the other end of his stall you will find huge mounds of roasted nuts, dried apricots, prunes, raisins and the most delicious crystallised fruits and sweetmeats. Everything you could possibly want for a tasty apéritif or as culinary condiments.

600 g (1 lb 5 oz) BLACK OLIVES
A LARGE SPRIG FRESH FENNEL
2 TEASPOONS DRIED THYME
2 TEASPOONS DRIED ROSEMARY
2 TEASPOONS DRIED SAVORY
2 BAY LEAVES
2 TEASPOONS FENNEL SEEDS
400–500 ml (12–16 fl oz) EXTRA VIRGIN FIRST-PRESSING OLIVE OIL

Mix together the olives and herbs, except the fresh fennel, in a large glass bowl.

Place the fennel in an airtight 1-litre glass jar, and spoon in the olives mixed with the herbs. Pour over enough oil so that all the olives are covered. Seal the jar and store in a dry, cool place for 10 days before using.

To serve, take the olives out of the jar with a slotted spoon, so that the oil can drain from the fruit. Keep the oil to use in salad dressings.

NOTE: It is important to be aware that olives vary greatly in flavour, depending on their origin. French olives tend to be fruity, often with a subtle nutty nuance. Greek olives are quite sharp and much stronger. Spanish olives are generally very mild. The same applies to olive oils. So it helps always to look for the varieties of olives and olive oils that complement your palate.

GREEN OLIVES

OLIVES VERTES

Shortly after the grape harvest, when everyone has had a little time to recover, there is another sort of harvesting to be done. This time it is the green olives that are picked. By then the days have turned slightly toward autumn and there is little cause to rush. So a gentler pace is engaged in this convivial pastime. We choose a bright, sunny afternoon, load a tall ladder onto the car along with various buckets and cloth bags for gathering the olives, and off we go. The best variety from our region are the Lucques, plump and longish in form with a pointed end, and quite delicate and nutty in flavour. We usually gather about 10–15 kg, which takes us the better part of an afternoon.

It is possible to buy freshly picked, untreated olives in the local markets for a short time in autumn, but somehow it never seems right to cure them without having taken part in the initial picking process. The recipe below is only one way of curing green olives. It is rather long, but the final results make all that effort worth the taking. Take note, caustic soda burns — handle it with great care and respect.

NOTE: Ripe black olives require another curing method.

15 kg (33 lb) FRESH GREEN OLIVES
15–18 LITRES (30–36 PINTS) COLD WATER
1 LITRE (2 PINTS) CAUSTIC SODA (15-20% SOLUTION)
1 kg (2 lb 4 oz) COARSE-GRAINED SEA SALT

FOR THE BRINE

100 g (4 oz) COARSE-GRAINED SEA SALT PER LITRE OF
WATER

All olives, whether green or ripe (black), are inedible when raw due to a substance called glycoside, which is abundant in their flesh. In order to eat this wonderful fruit, therefore, it is essential to leach out the bitterness before the final preparation. Using caustic soda may sound drastic to some, but it is very quick and effective, and with care and patience your cured olives will be delicious.

Take a large plastic or stainless steel container outside to an area where there is safe drainage. Fill it with 15–18 litres (26–31 pints) of water.

Sort through the olives to make sure none are damaged, and that none have worm holes in them. Take care how you handle them, as they do bruise easily.

With old clothes on, rubber gloves and safety glasses, add the caustic soda solution very carefully to the water. Stir with a piece of wood to mix well, then gently tip the olives into the solution. Leave for 6–8 hours, stirring from time to time. The length of time depends on the size of the olives; if they are less fleshy, it will take less time for them to cure. Ideally, you want the solution to work through to about 1 mm from the stone of the olive. You will see by slicing the flesh off one side of the olive how the colour changes between where the solution has penetrated the flesh of the olive and where it has not.

When the olives are cured, drain off the solution very carefully and dispose of it safely. Rinse everything, including the area you have been working, with copious amounts of running water.

Refill the container with cold water, so that the olives are floating freely, and leave them to soak overnight. In the morning, change the water and throw in a fistful of coarse sea salt. Do this 3 times a day for between 4 and 6 days, until all the caustic solution has been thoroughly rinsed away. You will be able to tell this by the clarity of the water, and the fact that the olives will have lost their soapy feeling.

To make the brine, boil enough water and salt for the quantity of olives you have — allow about 500ml (1 pint) of water for each 1-litre jar of olives. Leave to cool overnight. Put the olives in glass jars, pour the brine over them and seal. Wipe the jars with a damp cloth and store in a dark, dry place. The olives will keep for up to a year in their brine. You can also add herbs like fennel and spices to the brine if you wish.

MUSHROOMS BRAISED IN OIL, WITH PARSLEY AND GARLIC

CHAMPIGNONS À LA PERSILLADE

SERVES 4

500 g (1 lb 2 oz) FIELD MUSHROOMS, WIPED AND SLICED
4 TABLESPOONS OLIVE OIL FOR THE PAN AND
APPROXIMATELY 50 ml (2 fl oz) FOR THE MARINADE
SALT AND PEPPER

FOR THE PERSILLADE

2 LARGE CLOVES GARLIC
1 BUNCH FLAT-LEAFED PARSLEY

Put the sliced mushrooms into a glass bowl, drizzle a little olive oil over them, season with salt and pepper, and leave them to marinate for about 1 hour.

Heat olive oil in a heavy-bottomed frying pan. Drain the mushrooms of the marinating oil and sauté them gently in the fresh oil.

In the meantime, to make the persillade, chop the garlic and parsley together until quite fine. Toss this mixture over the mushrooms, sauté for 3–4 minutes more, and serve piping hot.

GARLIC SOUP

AÏGO BOULIDO

A wonderfully reviving soup. Legend has it that it will ward off all manner of ills, cure hangovers and cleanse the blood. As well as all that, it tastes delicious and will not leave you reeking of garlic.

SERVES 4

1 LITRE (2 PINTS) WATER
6 CLOVES GARLIC, CRUSHED IN THEIR SKINS
1 BAY LEAF
1 BRANCH SAGE LEAVES
2 TABLESPOONS OLIVE OIL
SALT AND PEPPER
4 ROUNDS BAGUETTE
2 EGG YOLKS
A LITTLE GRATED GRUYÈRE OR CHOPPED PARSLEY
TO GARNISH

In a saucepan, bring the water to boil and add the crushed garlic, bay leaf, sage leaves, olive oil, a little salt and pepper. Cover and simmer for 15 minutes.

While the stock is cooking, toast the rounds of baguette and put them into 4 warmed soup ramekins.

Remove the herbs and garlic from the stock with a slotted spoon. In a soup tureen, beat the egg yolks thoroughly. Slowly add the stock to the beaten eggs, whisking all the while. Spoon over the toasted baguette, and sprinkle with a little gruyère or chopped parsley, if you wish.

WALNUT SOUP

SOUPE AUX NOIX

When the grapes and the green olives have been harvested, we are also fortunate enough to enjoy our fair share of fresh walnuts. The main growing areas in France for this rich, oily nut are in the Perigord and around Grenoble, but the tree will grow in most regions here, and we have several down by the river in our village.

After an agreeable walk in the late afternoon sun we can return to the house, pockets bulging, and feast on our spoils or add a few tablespoonfuls to this delicate soup, which everyone seems to enjoy.

SERVES 4

4 LARGE FLOURY POTATOES, SLICED
2 ONIONS, SLICED
500 ml (16 fl oz) CHICKEN STOCK
2 HEAPED TABLESPOONS CRUSHED WALNUTS
250 ml (8 fl oz) CREAM
2 TABLESPOONS LEMON JUICE
SALT AND PEPPER TO TASTE
2 TABLESPOONS CHOPPED CHIVES OR PARSLEY

Place the potatoes and onions in a saucepan and pour over the stock. Simmer until the vegetables are cooked. Leave to cool, then place the mixture with the walnuts in a food processor or blender and process until smooth.

Pour back into the saucepan, reheat and add the cream and lemon juice 10 minutes before serving. Spoon over the chopped chives or parsley to garnish.

SAUSAGE MEAT TARTLETS

TARTELETTES À LA SAUCISSE

The first time we tasted these divine little tartlets was after three long weeks of hard slog, picking grapes during the grape harvest. At the end of the harvest, the tradition here is to have a *soulenque* (harvest feast) for all those who have taken part. After a generous number of apéritifs accompanied by big bowls of home-cured green olives, we were seated at an enormously long table on which were placed large platters, crammed with warm sausage-meat tartlets, enough to feed Napoleon's legionnaires. A simple salad followed, of sharp-tasting frisée greens with a walnut dressing, and that was just the entrée!

SERVES 6

250 g (9 oz) PÂTE BRISÉE (SEE PAGE 121)
2 TABLESPOONS OLIVE OIL
1 ONION, FINELY CHOPPED
1 kg (2 lb 4 oz) MINCED PURE PORK, NOT TRIMMED
OF ITS FAT
1 TABLESPOON HEAPED WHITE FLOUR
200 g (7 oz) CRÈME FRAÎCHE
SALT AND PEPPER TO SEASON

Make the pastry in advance and line either a large, 30-cm (12-inch), tart tin or, if you have them, six 10-cm (4-inch) tartlet tins. Bake blind for 10 minutes in a hot oven, 215°C (425°F; gas mark 7).

For the filling, in a frying pan, sauté the onion in a little olive oil until opaque. Add the pork and cook on a gentle heat until it starts to go golden, stirring all the while.

Sprinkle the flour evenly over the meat, again stirring so that it does not catch. Add the crème fraîche and continue cooking slowly until the meat and the sauce combine well and the sauce has thickened. Season with salt and pepper and spoon the mixture into the pastry cases. Return them to the oven and cook for a further 10–15 minutes, until bubbling and slightly golden on top. Serve hot or warm.

PORK LIVER PÂTÉ OF SOUTH-WEST FRANCE

FRICANDEAU

This delicious pâté is always available in our local charcuterie and is enjoyed by many in our region. It is simple to make, though the process is perhaps a little lengthy, but it is worth it. There are three ways it can be prepared: sterilised in glass preserving jars for keeping, or cooked in the oven in either terrines or balls wrapped in caul. The latter is how our first-rate charcutier prepares his. Caul is a very fine membrane veined with fat that encloses the stomach of animals. In French charcuterie cooking it is often pigs' caul that is used. It is soaked in water to soften it a little and wrapped around meats, terrines and pâtés to hold the ingredients together and keeps them moist during cooking. It is extremely useful and has no flavour or texture once cooked. The quantities below are for conserving and making 10 350-g (12-oz) jars. For a smaller quantity for making terrines, halve or quarter the recipe.

1 kg (2 lb 4 oz) FRESH PORK BREAST OR BELLY, MINCED
1 kg (2 lb 4 oz) PORK LIVER, MINCED
1 kg (2 lb 4 oz) WHITE PORK LARD, MINCED
CAUL IF YOU ARE MAKING FRICANDEAU BALLS
(ASK YOUR BUTCHER FOR THIS)
20 g (1 oz) FINE SALT PER 1 kg OF MEAT MIXTURE
2 g GROUND PEPPER PER 1 kg OF MEAT MIXTURE

Cut the meat, liver and lard into strips and pass through a mincer if your butcher cannot do this for you. Mix all of this together well, along with the seasoning.

FOR PRESERVING IN GLASS JARS: Divide the mixture evenly between the ten 350-g (12-oz) jars and close with new seals. Place the jars in a sterilising pan (you may need to do it in two lots), taking care to separate the jars with old rags so that they do not bang against each other when boiling. Place a brick or heavy weight on top of each jar and fill the pan with cold water until the lids are well under water. Make sure there is enough room in the pan for the water to boil without boiling over. Turn the heat up high until the water begins to boil and maintain this for 2 hours.

After 2 hours' steady boiling, turn the heat off and leave to cool until the following morning. Remove the jars and wipe, checking that the seals are firm and airtight as you go. Store in a cool, dry place for up to 6 months.

FOR BAKING IN A TERRINE: Preheat water in a shallow bain-marie in a moderate oven, 180°C (350°F; gas mark 4). Line an ovenproof terrine dish with caul and spoon in the meat mixture, spreading it out evenly. Wrap the caul over the top. Replace the lid and cook in the bain-marie at 180°C for 1¹/₂–2 hours. When cooked, allow to cool before placing it in the refrigerator for a minimum of 12 hours before serving.

FOR BAKING IN BALLS IN A ROASTING DISH: This is almost the same procedure as for a terrine, except that you roll the meat mixture into balls about the size of a grapefruit or orange, and then wrap the balls in caul. Place them symmetrically next to one another in the roasting dish. Cook in a moderate oven, 180°C (350°F; gas mark 4), for 1¹/₂–2 hours.

NOTE: When baking the pâté, cooking times will vary according to the amount of mixture you make. In all cases, serve cold in slices with cornichons (gherkins) and chunky rye bread, or a crisp, green salad.

HOT SALAD OF GREEN LENTILS

SALADE CHAUDE AUX LENTILLES

A delicious and highly nutritious way of cooking green lentils. Although this is a hot salad, it is equally tasty cold the next day.

SERVES 4

500 g (1 lb 2 oz) GREEN LENTILS, PREFERABLY
PUY DE DÔME VARIETY
1 ONION, WHOLE, PEELED AND STUCK WITH 2 CLOVES
A BOUQUET GARNI OF 1 BAY LEAF, A BUNCH OF FRESH
THYME AND PARSLEY
3–4 PEPPERCORNS
1 SMALL CARROT, DICED
200 g (7 oz) LARDONS OR CHOPPED BACON
1 LARGE RIPE FIRM TOMATO, DICED
CHOPPED PARSLEY, TO GARNISH

FOR THE VINAIGRETTE

50 g (2 oz) OLIVE OIL
25 g (1 oz) RED-WINE VINEGAR
1 CLOVE GARLIC, CRUSHED
SALT IF NEEDED

Place the lentils in a saucepan, cover with cold water and bring to the boil. When the water is boiling, add the onion, bouquet garni, peppercorns and carrot. Cover and simmer gently for 45–60 minutes. The cooking time will depend on the freshness of the lentils. Ideally, they should still be slightly firm when cooked, and not mushy.

While the lentils are cooking, sauté the bacon or lardons until slightly golden, and make up the vinaigrette.

When the lentils are cooked, drain them well and place in a warmed dish. Discard the bouquet garni and onion. Add the bacon or lardons and the chopped tomato, and pour over the vinaigrette. Sprinkle with chopped parsley and toss well.

This salad can be eaten on its own, or as an accompaniment, and is very good served with fatty meats as the lentils lessen fatty tastes and textures.

SPICED MUSHROOMS

CHAMPIGNONS ÉPICÉS

During the autumn months our local pharmacy always has a huge poster pinned up, displaying the many varieties of wild mushrooms to be found in our region. And it is not uncommon to see one of *les anciens* arriving on his bicycle nursing a basket of foreign-looking fungi for the pharmacist to check out, to determine whether or not they are edible. In fact, you could go as far as to say that mushrooming is a national sport in France. After all, anything worth eating is worth seeking out. Despite all the charts and advice, mushroom poisoning is not uncommon, so we prefer to stick to the cultivated varieties, of which there are many; occasionally we strike it lucky on a Sunday afternoon stroll and return with a bag of chanterelle or cèpe mushrooms.

SERVES 4

500 g (1 lb 2 oz) BUTTON MUSHROOMS
50 ml (2 fl oz) OLIVE OIL
100 ml (3 fl oz) WHITE WINE
1 TEASPOON GROUND CUMIN SEEDS
1 TEASPOON GROUND CORIANDER
4 LARGE CLOVES GARLIC, CRUSHED
JUICE OF A LEMON
SALT AND PEPPER
A GOOD HANDFUL FLAT-LEAFED PARSLEY

In a heavy-based frying pan, heat the olive oil and add the mushrooms. Let them cook for a few minutes, stirring gently, then add the white wine, spices, garlic and a little water, if need be. Simmer gently for about 10–15 minutes, until the mushrooms are almost ready. Pour in the lemon juice and season with salt. Continue to cook quickly to reduce the juice, if need be. Just before serving, stir in the chopped parsley. Turn out into a warmed earthenware bowl, and serve with wholemeal toast or accompanying roasted or grilled meat.

POACHED VEAL IN WHITE SAUCE
BLANQUETTE DE VEAU

Any good, self-respecting French café, bistro or brasserie will always feature this much-loved classic on their weekly menu. When cooked well it is to die for. It was not until a Parisienne friend passed on her family recipe that I had real success with cooking it myself. Now it features regularly on our menu too. The cuts of veal best used for this dish are either the shoulder, breast or neck pieces. As a variation, the veal can be replaced with lamb and the mushrooms with new season's asparagus tips. In the interests of time it is perfectly feasible to make it in advance and reheat.

SERVES 4

600 g (1 lb 5 oz) BONED SHOULDER, BREAST OR NECK OF VEAL, CUT INTO LARGE PIECES
100 g (3 oz) BABY WHITE ONIONS, OR 1 LARGE ONION CUT INTO QUARTERS
1 LARGE CARROT, SPLIT AND CUT INTO QUARTERS
A BOUQUET GARNI OF BAY, THYME AND FLAT-LEAFED PARSLEY
SALT AND PEPPER TO SEASON
30 g (1 oz) UNSALTED BUTTER
25 g (1 oz) FLOUR
1 EGG YOLK
2 TABLESPOONS COLD MILK
125 g (4 oz) BUTTON OR CHANTERELLE MUSHROOMS, LIGHTLY SAUTÉED (DRIED AND RECONSTITUTED WILL DO)
JUICE OF A LEMON
100 g (3 oz) CRÈME FRAÎCHE

Place the pieces of veal in a large saucepan and cover with cold water. Bring to the boil, add the onions, carrot and bouquet garni, and season with salt and pepper. Reduce the heat to a steady simmer, cover, and leave to cook for 75–90 minutes, depending on the cut of meat you have used. The breast will take slightly longer to cook than the neck or shoulder pieces. When ready, drain the meat and vegetables, keeping the bouillon (stock) that you have cooked it in. Discard the bouquet garni and put the meat and vegetables to one side for the moment.

In the same saucepan, over a low heat, melt the butter and add the flour. Stirring so that it does not burn, let this roux cook for 3–4 minutes on a low heat then start to add the bouillon little by little, stirring all the time, until you have a good white sauce. Let this cook slowly for 10–15 minutes.

While the sauce is cooking, beat the egg yolk with the cold milk in a bowl, then add a little of the white sauce to the egg and milk mixture. Whisk, then add this mixture to the white sauce, raise the heat and stir vigorously with a whisk until the sauce begins to boil. After 1–2 minutes reduce the heat again. Taste the sauce and adjust the seasoning if need be. Return the meat to the sauce and add the mushrooms.

If you are making the Blanquette de Veau in advance, it is at this point that you would leave the dish to cool and refrigerate until ready to use.

Just prior to serving add the lemon juice and crème fraîche. Serve with steamed potatoes, and slices of fresh baguette to mop up the sauce.

NOTE: If you are using dried mushrooms, they need to be soaked in warm water for an hour prior to use and washed and drained at least twice.

CASSEROLE OF VEAL WITH GREEN OLIVES

VEAU EN COCOTTE AUX OLIVES VERTES

A superb dish with a tangy marriage of flavours that blend well without overpowering your tastebuds. We love it best cooked in the autumn, using the newly harvested green olives and simple button mushrooms.

SERVES 4

1 kg (2 lb 4 oz) SHOULDER VEAL, CUT INTO LARGE CUBES
100 g (3 oz) BACON, FAT AND RIND REMOVED, DICED
2 LARGE ONIONS, PEELED AND QUARTERED, OR
15 SMALL ONIONS, PEELED
2 CLOVES GARLIC, CRUSHED UNDER THE BLADE OF A KNIFE
4 LARGE SPRIGS OF FRESH SAGE (OR 2 TEASPOONS DRIED SAGE)

45 ml (2 fl oz) TOMATO PURÉE
350 ml (12 fl oz) DRY WHITE WINE
200–300 ml (7–11 fl oz) STOCK, PREFERABLY VEAL
2 HANDFULS GREEN OLIVES, PITTED
200 g (7 oz) FRESH BUTTON MUSHROOMS
SALT AND PEPPER TO TASTE

Take a heavy-based cast-iron casserole dish, and pack in the veal, bacon, onions, garlic and sage leaves.

Mix the tomato purée with the wine and enough stock so that the combined liquids just cover the meat. Bring to the boil, reduce the heat slightly, and simmer gently for 1 hour.

Add the green olives and cook for a further 30 minutes, or until the meat is tender. Add the mushrooms, season and leave for another 10–15 minutes.

Serve with wide buttered noodles or boiled potatoes and triangles of fried French bread.

SAUTÉ OF VEAL

SAUTÉ DE VEAU

This is a simple and delicious way of cooking veal, but it can just as easily be made with lamb or chicken. The basic principle of a sauté is that the meat is first browned, then cooked in a shallow-sided sauté pan on top of the stove over a brisk heat. A little liquid is then added, usually wine or stock, some flour, and the pan is covered until the meat is cooked. The sauce is created in the pan while the dish cooks, with the juices of the meat, the flour and the wine, which gives the dish a beautifully rounded, intense flavour.

SERVES 4

2–3 TABLESPOONS OLIVE OIL
700 g (1 lb 9 oz) SHOULDER OF VEAL, CUT INTO
LARGE CUBES
1 LARGE ONION, SLICED THINLY
2 CLOVES GARLIC, CRUSHED
1 TABLESPOON FLOUR
150 ml (5 fl oz) DRY WHITE WINE
1 LARGE RED PEPPER, GRILLED, PEELED AND SLICED
500 g (1 lb 2 oz) TOMATOES, PEELED, SEEDED AND
CHOPPED
SALT AND PEPPER TO SEASON

In a shallow-sided sauté pan, heat the olive oil, and brown the cubes of meat on all sides. Remove to a side plate with a slotted spoon. Cook the onion and garlic for 3 minutes.

Place the meat back in the pan with the onions and garlic, and sprinkle over the flour. Stir well and add the white wine. Add the sliced red pepper, the tomatoes and season with salt and pepper. Cover and allow to cook gently for 50–75 minutes, until the meat is tender. Serve very hot with Caramelised Turnips (see page 111), carrots and potatoes.

LEEKS AND HAM IN WHITE SAUCE

POIREAUX ET JAMBON À LA BÉCHAMEL

A great luncheon or light supper dish and a nutritious winter meal. As an alternative to leeks, Belgian endive can be used or 2–3 Brussels sprouts per person.

SERVES 4

4 MEDIUM-SIZED LEEKS, TRIMMED AND CLEANED
4 SLICES WHITE HAM
2–3 KNOBS BUTTER
SALT AND PEPPER
50 g (2 oz) GRUYÈRE CHEESE (OPTIONAL)

FOR THE BÉCHAMEL SAUCE

40 g (1.5 oz) BUTTER
40 g (1.5 oz) FLOUR
500 ml (16 fl oz) MILK
1/2 TEASPOON SALT TO SEASON
SPRINKLING OF GROUND NUTMEG

To make the sauce, gently melt the butter in a saucepan. Add the flour and stir briskly, allowing the roux to cook on a low heat for 2–3 minutes without burning.

Begin adding the milk little by little, whisking as you go so that any lumps that may form are beaten out. Continue to add the milk and stir constantly as the sauce thickens. Ideally the mixture should be the texture of thick cream when it is ready. Season with salt and nutmeg. Turn off the heat and put to one side.

Butter a good-sized gratin dish. Boil a saucepan of salted water and blanch the leeks quickly. Remove from the water and pat dry. Wrap each leek in a slice of ham and arrange in the buttered gratin dish. Season with salt and pepper if required. Pour the béchamel sauce over the leeks and ham and sprinkle over the gruyere, if you wish.

Place in a moderate oven, 180°C (350°F; gas mark 4), and cook for 30–40 minutes, until cooked through and nicely golden on top.

BRAISED PHEASANT ON A BED OF RED CABBAGE

ESTOUFFADE DE FAISAN SUR LIT DE CHOU ROUGE

A cocotte is the French name for a deep, heavy-based cast-iron casserole dish, which can be used either on top of the stove or in the oven. Much of the country-style or *familiale* cooking found in rural France employs this indispensable cooking vessel. They come in various shapes and sizes, often big enough to fit a whole chicken or hare. And they are perfect for slowly braising meat and vegetables, or both, in their own juices, with just a little wine added. They are particularly useful for cooking game, as the slow, covered, moist cooking helps to stop the meat from drying out.

SERVES 6

A BRACE OF YOUNG PHEASANTS, PLUCKED, DRAWN AND OVEN-READY
3 TABLESPOONS LIGHT OLIVE OIL
1 SMALL RED CABBAGE, SLICED COARSELY
1 RED PEPPER, ROASTED, SEEDED AND SKINNED, THEN SLICED INTO STRIPS
250 ml (8 fl oz) GOOD-QUALITY CLARET-STYLE RED WINE
A FEW TABLESPOONS OF GOOD STOCK OR CANNED GAME CONSOMMÉ
SALT AND PEPPER

Warm the olive oil in a heavy-based, cast-iron casserole dish, and brown the birds on all sides. Remove the birds and put to one side.

Add the red cabbage to the casserole and coat it in the cooking juices by stirring well as it cooks. Add the slices of red capsicum. Raise the heat and return the birds to the casserole, placing them on the bed of red cabbage. Pour over the red wine and stock. Season with salt and pepper, and seal the casserole (a piece of foil placed over the opening before putting the lid on is easiest). Cook in a moderate oven, 180°C (350°F; gas mark 4), for 40–50 minutes, until the birds are tender but still moist.

NOTE: The time for cooking a pheasant in this way can be roughly estimated as for cooking a chicken. However, if you were to roast the birds, they would need to be cooked quickly, in a hot oven, 215°C (420°F; gas mark 7), so that they do not dry out.

QUAIL WITH SHERRY VINEGAR

CAILLES AU VINAIGRE DE XÉRÈS

The quail is a small migratory bird usually found in flat open country. Once abundant in Europe, it has become more and more rare. So the majority of quail cooked today are farm-raised. The birds are plump-chested and the flesh full of flavour. It is a marvellous bird for cooking, very versatile, and as delicious simply grilled with fresh herbs on a wood-fire barbecue as done in a sauce, stuffed or as a pâté. At Les Mimosas quail feature regularly on the menu in a variety of ways.

SERVES 4

4 QUAIL, CLEANED AND TRUSSED
3–4 TABLESPOONS OLIVE OIL
1 GOOD BUNCH FRESH THYME
60 ml (2 fl oz) SHERRY VINEGAR
250 ml (8 fl oz) FRESH CREAM (OPTIONAL)

Set the oven to a high heat, 215°C (425°F; gas mark 7). In a casserole, heat the oil, brown the quail quickly then set aside. Reduce the heat slightly and add the fresh thyme to the casserole. Arrange the quail on top of the thyme, pour in the sherry vinegar, and simmer steadily for 3 minutes.

Cover the casserole and place in the hot oven to finish cooking — about 15–20 minutes. When cooked the quail should still be pink but the meat firm. Serve the quail whole on a bed of fresh thyme with the juices of the casserole spooned over the birds.

A cup of fresh cream may be added to the cooking juices 5 minutes prior to serving, if desired.

TROUT IN MARROW

TRUITE À LA COURGE

The traditional method for this dish is to cook the trout in a cavity scooped out of the marrow, so that the cooking juices are absorbed by the marrow, and produce an extraordinary combination of tastes. The problem arises, when cooking for many, of finding a marrow large enough to hold the trout. Here is an alternative which overcomes that problem and works equally well.

SERVES 4

1.5–2 kg (3–4 lb 8 oz) FRESH TROUT, GUTTED AND WASHED
3 kg (6 lb 12 oz) MARROW
2–3 CLOVES GARLIC, CRUSHED
2–3 TABLESPOONS OLIVE OIL
GROUND BLACK PEPPER AND SALT, TO TASTE

Cut the marrow into slices 2.5 cm (1 inch) thick and remove the skin. Lay half the slices in a large baking pan. Lay the trout over the top of the marrow. Sprinkle over the garlic and olive oil, season with pepper and salt. Spread a second layer of marrow over the trout. Cover all of this with a sheet of cooking foil.

Preheat the oven to 180°C (350°F; gas mark 4). Cook for 45–60 minutes, until you can pull out the dorsal fins without difficulty — this is the most precise way of finding out how well the fish is cooked. Remove from the oven and serve the trout surrounded by the marrow, with the cooking juices.

PIGEONS BRAISED ON BROWN RICE WITH HERBS

PIGEONS EN COCOTTE

Pigeon is one of the most satisfying of game birds to eat, with its dark, dense breast flesh and delicately gamey flavour. The best birds to eat are wild pigeon — although, of course, not the protected New Zealand native pigeon — but nowadays pigeons are raised commercially; although still very good, they lack the depth of flavour that a wild pigeon has. For the sake of convenience, in this recipe we have used the commercially raised variety, but if you can get hold of wild wood pigeon — bravo! One medium-sized bird is ample for one person.

SERVES 4

4 MEDIUM-SIZED, OVEN-READY PIGEONS

FOR EACH BIRD

1 TEASPOON MARC DE BOURGOGNE
3 SPRIGS EACH FRESH THYME, ROSEMARY AND OREGANO
55 g (2 oz) BUTTER

FOR THE RICE

200 g (7 oz) SMOKED STREAKY BACON
2 SHALLOTS, CHOPPED FINELY
SALT AND PEPPER
450 g (1 lb) BROWN RICE
850 ml (24 fl oz) CHICKEN OR VEAL STOCK

Into the cavity of each bird put a teaspoon of marc de Bourgogne, and roll the bird around so that the marc coats the interior. Then put a sprig of each herb into the cavity. Make sure there are no stray feathers left around the legs, neck and breast.

In a cast-iron casserole, melt the butter and sauté the streaky bacon and shallots for several minutes. Remove with a slotted spoon to a side plate. Next add the pigeons, one by one, turning them in the butter and browning all sides, making sure that the butter does not burn. Lift the pigeons out of the casserole and onto a plate. Season well with salt and pepper.

Add the brown rice to the butter, along with the shallots and bacon, stirring as you go. Pour in the stock and bring to the boil. Place the seasoned pigeons on top of the rice and arrange any remaining herbs around the birds. Cover and cook in a moderate oven, 180°C (350°F; gas mark 4), for approximately 1¹/₂ hours (this will depend slightly on the size of the birds you are cooking), until the pigeons are tender, and the rice is fluffy and has absorbed all its cooking juices.

NOTE: If you find it difficult to obtain pigeon, this dish will be almost as delicious with quail, poussin, young guinea fowl, pheasant or chicken. You may need to adjust the cooking time, however, depending on the size of the bird.

RABBIT IN PUFF PASTRY

LAPIN EN CROÛTE

Another divine way of cooking rabbit. The pastry case seals the casserole, and captures the essence of all the flavours inside the lid. This can also be done successfully with chicken.

RABBIT SELLERS AT CASTRES MARKET PROUDLY DISPLAY THEIR PRODUCE OF THE DAY

SERVES 4

1 MEDIUM-SIZED, OVEN-READY RABBIT, JOINTED
3 TABLESPOONS OLIVE OIL
2 SHALLOTS, FINELY CHOPPED
2 CLOVES GARLIC, FLATTENED UNDER THE BLADE OF A KNIFE
150–200 ml (5–7 fl oz) WHITE WINE
1 SMALL BUNCH THYME
1 TOMATO, SKINNED, SEEDED AND CHOPPED
SEA SALT AND BLACK PEPPER TO SEASON
200 g (7 oz) PUFF PASTRY

Heat the olive oil in an ovenproof casserole dish. Sauté the shallots until slightly soft, about 5 minutes. Remove

to a side plate with a slotted spoon. Throw in the garlic, and brown the rabbit pieces on both sides. Return the shallots to the casserole dish, and while the heat is high, pour over the wine. Let it cook for about 4–5 minutes. Add the thyme and chopped tomato to the casserole. Turn off the heat, season with freshly ground sea salt and black pepper.

Roll out the puff pastry on a floured surface. Carefully place the pastry over the contents of the casserole, and place in a fairly hot oven, 200°C (400°F; gas mark 6), for about 40 minutes. When the pastry is well browned and has risen, the meat will be ready. Serve immediately.

79

SAINT ANDRÉ TRIPE

TRIPES À LA SAINT ANDRÉ

There are two schools of thought when it comes to tripe — you either love it or you do not. I belonged to the latter school until coming to live in France, mainly because my youthful memories of tripe were of the whole house reeking of this foul-textured substance while it bubbled away on the stove, and we children knew we were in for a meal of furry rubber with, as far as we could see, no flavour at all.

Not so in France, where tripe is considered a delicacy by many and appears in numerous forms on restaurant menus, already prepared on supermarket shelves, preserved in pretty glass jars, and of course in people's homes. In our village it is the traditional dish served every autumn for the Fête de Saint André on 30 November, and our friends in the village usually have a pot of this amazing concoction simmering ever so sedately on their open hearth for three days prior to its consumption. The finished product is superb, we can vouch for that! Unlike my childhood experiences — sorry Ma.

The recipe that follows was generously given to us by our village friends but we have adapted it for cooking on the stove in a much shorter time. A word of warning when preparing and cooking tripe: make sure the raw product is washed thoroughly with a capital T, and that your kitchen is well ventilated to get rid of the strong odours while the dish is cooking. Tripe is also best cooked in a large quantity; what is not consumed can either be frozen or eaten the following day.

SERVES 8

2 kg (4 lb 8 oz) TRIPE, THOROUGHLY WASHED
2 CALVES' FEET, CUT LENGTHWAYS (ASK YOUR BUTCHER
TO DO THIS FOR YOU)
1 HAM HOCK
1 HEAPED TEASPOON TOMATO CONCENTRATE
2 WHOLE CORMS GARLIC, CLEANED AND PEELED
1 TABLESPOON DUCK FAT (IF YOU HAVE IT)

SALT
10 PEPPERCORNS
2 BAY LEAVES

FOR WASHING THE TRIPE

9 TABLESPOONS VINEGAR
SALT

Wash the raw tripe well, at least 2–3 times, in warm water that has 3 tablespoons of vinegar and a handful of salt in it each time. It will stand a good scrubbing. When it is clean, cut it into pieces about 2 cm (1 inch) square, and place in a decent-sized stockpot along with the split calves' feet. Cover with cold water and bring to the boil.

When the water has boiled, drain it off and refill the pot until the water covers the contents. Add to this the ham hock, tomato concentrate, garlic, duck fat if you have it, salt, peppercorns and bay leaves. Bring to a gentle simmer, cover, and leave to cook slowly for 5–6 hours. The tripe is ready when it is tender to the touch of a fork. Serve with steamed potatoes or fresh haricot beans.

FRENCH OMELETTE

OMELETTE AUX DEUX OEUFS

When I was growing up, an omelette was always this light fluffy yellow object that appeared in front of me on a plate at about the same height as my nose. It rather resembled a savoury version of candy floss in consistency, and was often made by my father, if I recall correctly.

I was delighted to rediscover this childhood favourite when we visited a restaurant near Mont St Michel in Normandy, where this type of omelette is a great speciality, cooked over a wood fire. I, unfortunately, was never as deft with this style of omelette-making as my Dad, so it was with more than a sigh of relief that I discovered English doyenne of the French provincial kitchen, Elizabeth David's, way of cooking omelettes, and managed to master this classic form of French omelette.

Add whatever extra flavours you like to it, be it mushrooms, cheese or herbs, but never use more than two eggs per person and do not beat the mixture. The other secret is to make sure your pan is spotlessly clean. The best way to clean an omelette pan is to fill the base with fine salt and heat the pan so that whatever is left in the pan is absorbed by the salt. Discard the salt and wipe the interior with a paper towel. Now you are ready to make your omelette.

SERVES 1

2 EGGS
GENEROUS KNOB UNSALTED BUTTER
GROUND BLACK PEPPER AND SALT, TO TASTE

Make sure your frying pan is clean; a non-stick pan is fine.

Crack 2 eggs into a bowl, add some freshly ground pepper and salt, and stir gently with a fork to break the yolks and mix with the whites. Do not beat the eggs.

Put a generous knob of good quality, unsalted butter in the frying pan and place on a high heat. When the butter is almost burning, tip in the eggs and push the mixture towards the centre as it starts to cook, allowing the liquid eggs to fill the spaces. You can do this with a fork and lift the pan on an angle as you do it.

Lower the heat and allow the eggs to cook to your liking; some people like their omelette a little runny on top, others prefer it well cooked.

OPTIONAL: At this stage you can add whatever filling you prefer to one half of the omelette. When cooked, fold the omelette over and slide it onto a hot plate. Garnish to your preference. I am a bit of a traditionalist, so for me chopped parsley is hard to beat.

PAN-SAUTÉED POTATOES
POMMES DE TERRE À LA POÊLE

A favourite way of preparing potatoes with the French. In the south, the preferred fats are olive oil, goose and duck fat, the latter being particularly delicious and definitely addictive. An ideal accompaniment to roasted or grilled meats.

SERVES 4

750 g (1 lb 10 oz) WAXY POTATOES, PEELED
AND CUT INTO CUBES
1 TABLESPOON BUTTER AND 3 TABLESPOONS OLIVE OIL
OR
50 g (2 oz) DUCK, GOOSE OR PORK FAT (DUCK
OR GOOSE IS BEST)
2 CLOVES GARLIC, PEELED
A GOOD HANDFUL OF PARSLEY, PREFERABLY
THE FLAT-LEAFED VARIETY
SEA SALT AND BLACK PEPPER

Boil the potatoes in salted water until almost tender. Drain and leave to cool.

In a sauté pan, heat the oil and butter or fat, and brown the potatoes evenly for about 10 minutes on a medium heat. Take care not to damage the potatoes as you turn them. Chop the parsley and garlic finely together, add to the potatoes and continue cooking for another 5 minutes or until nicely browned.

Turn out into a bowl and season with freshly ground sea salt and black pepper.

RICOTTA CAKE

GÂTEAU À LA RICOTTA

A cake to beat all cakes, this rich hedonist's delight makes a superb dessert. But be warned, a small slice will satisfy the most passionate sweet tooth.

FOR THE CRUST

375 g (12 oz) PLAIN FLOUR
3 TEASPOONS BAKING POWDER
150 g (5 oz) BROWN SUGAR
125 g (4 oz) ALMOND MEAL
1 EGG, LIGHTLY BEATEN
1 TEASPOON PURE VANILLA ESSENCE
250 g (9 oz) VERY COLD BUTTER, CUT INTO SMALL PIECES

FOR THE FILLING

800 g (1 lb 12 oz) RICOTTA CHEESE
85 g (3 oz) PINE NUTS, TOASTED
30 ml (1 fl oz) DARK RUM OR COGNAC
60 g (2 oz) DARK BITTER CHOCOLATE, CHOPPED FINELY
225 g (8 oz) CASTOR SUGAR

ICING SUGAR TO DECORATE

Make the crust first, by combining the flour, baking powder, sugar, almond meal, egg and vanilla in a large bowl. Rub in the butter until the mixture begins to look like breadcrumbs. Refrigerate for 30 minutes.

Line a 23-cm (9-inch) round springform tin with a single sheet of cooking foil, pressing it well into the sides. Butter the foil well.

In another bowl, prepare the filling by combining the ricotta, pine nuts, rum or cognac, chocolate and castor sugar.

Press half the crust mixture into the base of the prepared cake tin. Cover with the ricotta filling, then gently spoon over the remaining crust mixture, spreading it evenly.

Bake in a moderate oven, 180°C (350°F; gas mark 4), for approximately 1 hour, or until the cake has risen slightly and is golden brown in colour. When cooked, allow it to cool completely in the cake tin. When cool remove it from the tin, peel off the cooking foil and sieve a thick layer of icing sugar over the top of the cake. Slice and serve with a dob of crème fraîche.

WALNUT TART

TARTE AUX NOIX

Walnut tarts feature in many forms all over France. They are always decadently rich and always hard to say no to. On many southern market bakers' stalls you will find a very rich version with a ground walnut mixture baked between two layers of heavy, sweet pastry. Another version finds the walnuts mixed with almonds and lemon and layered between puff pastry, lighter though equally rich. This recipe sits somewhere in the middle.

SERVES 6

250 g (9 oz) PÂTE SABLÉE (SEE PAGE 121)
3 EGGS
350 g (12 oz) WALNUTS, CRUSHED INTO BITS
4 TABLESPOONS MILD HONEY
2 TABLESPOONS FULL CREAM (48% FAT)
PINCH NUTMEG AND CINNAMON
1–2 TEASPOONS ICING SUGAR

Make the pastry and line an oiled 26-cm (10-inch) tart tin. Bake the pastry blind in a hot oven, 215°C (425°F; gas mark 7), for 10 minutes.

For the filling, whisk the eggs and mix in the walnut bits, honey and cream. Add the cinnamon and nutmeg. Pour the mixture into the pastry case, and bake in a moderate oven, 180°C (350°F; gas mark 4), for 30 minutes, until the mixture is bubbling and slightly risen.

Allow to cool slightly, dust with icing sugar and serve just warm.

GREEN TOMATO JAM
CONFITURE DE TOMATES VERTES

Virtually every retired vigneron in our village has a potager or vegetable garden that most people would die for. They line the riverbank with meticulously kept rows of lettuces, aubergines, peas, beans, capsicums, potatoes, radishes and the biggest, juiciest tomatoes you could imagine. Early morning and late afternoon these cheery, nut-brown, nuggety old chaps can be found tilling the soil, watering and composting, harvesting and sowing. As summer turns to autumn their enormous tomato plants, which produce kilo after kilo of sun-ripened fruit, still manage to keep producing large quantities of tomatoes, but by then the sun has lost its potency and they just do not get ripe enough to use in the normal way. So after the grape and olive harvests there is still time before the first frosts to pick the larger green tomatoes for making jam. And it would have to be one of the most delectable confitures ever to grace the breakfast table.

3 kg (6 lb 12 oz) GREEN TOMATOES, WASHED AND
CHOPPED INTO EIGHTHS
400 ml (12 fl oz) WATER
JUICE OF 3 LEMONS
2.5 kg (5 lb 4 oz) BROWN SUGAR

Put the fruit into a spacious jamming pan, along with the water. Cook the fruit until it is soft and pulpy, usually about 25–40 minutes.

When the fruit is cooked add the lemon juice and the brown sugar and raise the heat, bringing the mixture to the boil as quickly as possible, stirring all the time.

Continue to boil rapidly — a rolling boil is best — until the fruit has reached the setting stage, anywhere between 10 and 30 minutes. It is best to start testing after 10 minutes. If you do not have a jamming thermometer, dribble a little of the mixture onto a chilled saucer, leave for a minute, then run your finger through the mixture. If wrinkles form on top of the mixture you can go ahead and pot it into jars. If not, keep boiling until the mixture reaches this stage. Pot in warm jars and seal.

PICKLED GREEN TOMATOES
TOMATES VERTES AU VINAIGRE

At the end of the tomato season, when there are still plenty of small, unripe tomatoes on the vines, it seems a great shame to throw them on the compost. Monsieur Jeaneau, one of the most prolific gardeners in the village, gave us this recipe which he says is Spanish in origin. The quantities given here are enough for a 1-litre glass preserving jar. Use the tomatoes to accompany cold meats and pâtés, as you would gherkins, and for adding to casseroles.

500 g (1 lb 2 oz) SMALL GREEN TOMATOES
1 SMALL RED CHILLI, SEEDED AND CHOPPED ROUGHLY,
OR LEFT WHOLE
1 BAY LEAF
1 TABLESPOON YELLOW MUSTARD SEEDS
6 WHOLE PEPPERCORNS
500–700 ml (16–24 fl oz) RED-WINE VINEGAR

Wash the tomatoes well, and place them in a sterilised 1-litre glass jar along with the chilli, bay, yellow mustard seeds and peppercorns.

In a saucepan, heat the vinegar until it boils. Allow to cool a little, then pour over the tomatoes until they are completely covered. Seal the jar and leave for 6 weeks before eating.

ORANGE WINE

VIN D'ORANGE

In France, *l'heure d'apéritif* is an all-important part of the day, even more so in summer. It is the time of day when, for a short while after a hard day's work, everyone can relax and unwind, exchange the latest news and gossip, watch the world go by, or just hang out. In the south, the habitual apéritif is Pastis, a light aniseed-flavoured drink to which one adds water and ice. It is surprisingly refreshing after a hot, dusty day. The other popular apéritifs are the *vins doux* or sweet wines of the Midi, like lightly chilled muscat, cartagène and grenache. These are highly alcoholic, and are taken in small glasses to tempt the gastric juices, rather like a glass of sherry or madeira.

In wine-growing regions, if you are invited to someone's home for an *apéro*, as it is commonly referred to, you will often find delights like home-made orange or walnut wine. These can easily be made with a white wine base, and keep well.

In the end, the choice of drink is least important; it is the time with people that counts most, and in many French bars the percentage of soft drinks and fruit syrups sold is as high as the alcoholic beverages.

5 ORANGES, PEELED
5–6 CAMOMILE FLOWERS
5 COFFEE BEANS
4 LITRES (8 PINTS) WHITE WINE
1 LITRE (2 PINTS) EAU-DE-VIE
1 kg (2 lb 4 oz) SUGAR
650 ml (20 fl oz) WATER

Clean a large glass container, like a flagon, with boiling water and dry well. Put the peeled oranges, camomile flowers and coffee beans into the glass vessel. Add the wine, then the eau-de-vie, stir well, seal, and leave this mixture to meld for 30 days.

At the end of this time, filter the contents and return them to the glass vessel. Make a syrup with the sugar and water, making sure that all the sugar is dissolved. Add this to the mixture before decanting it into bottles. Cork well, and leave for a good week before drinking.

TOP: DINNER ON THE BALCONY WITH VEAL CASSEROLE AND SAUTEED POTATOES
BOTTOM: AUTUMN VINEYARDS AFTER THE RUSH AND BUSTLE OF THE GRAPE HARVEST

WALNUT WINE

VIN DE NOIX

20 WALNUTS, CUT IN HALF AND CRUSHED
1 kg (2 lb 4 oz) SUGAR
750 ml (24 fl oz) EAU-DE-VIE
5 LITRES (10 PINTS) RED WINE AT 13–14% ALCOHOL

Clean a large glass vessel with boiling water, and dry well. Place the walnuts in the glass jar with the sugar, eau-de-vie and wine. Stir well.

Seal and leave the contents for 40 days, but stir each day. At the end of 40 days, filter and bottle.

QUINCE SWEETMEATS

PÂTE DE COINGS

An ancient and much-favoured fruit, the quince grows in most temperate climates. It resembles a pear, although the yellow fruit of this pretty tree is generally much bigger. In autumn when the fruit ripens the skin is covered in a fine, fuzzy down and the flesh is very hard and bitter to the taste, but full of pectin and tannin, making it ideal for jellies and sweetmeats. The latter is a traditional Christmas gift and is almost always among the 13 desserts featured at Provençal Christmas feasts.

1–2 kg (2 lb 8 oz) QUINCES
150 ml (5 fl oz) WATER FOR EVERY 1 kg OF FRUIT
SUGAR (SEE METHOD)
JUICE OF 1 LEMON

Rub off the fluff, wash the quinces and cut them into chunks without coring them. Place them in a jamming pan with the water. Bring to the boil and simmer until the fruit is soft and pulpy. You can use a potato masher to help mash the fruit once it is tender. When the fruit is very soft, pass it through a fine sieve and weigh the resulting pulp.

Return the pulp to the pan and add an equal weight of sugar, and the juice of the lemon. Stir over a gentle heat until all the sugar is dissolved.

Raise the heat slightly and continue to cook until the purée is thick and elastic, and pulls away easily from the side of the pan. The thicker it becomes, the more you will need to stir it to stop it catching and sticking.

Prepare a baking tray with baking paper and turn out the mass on to the tray, spreading it evenly with the help of a dampened spatula, to about 2 cm (1 inch) thick. Leave it to dry in a warm, dry spot; a hot water cupboard is ideal.

When it is dry and firm cut it into diamond shapes, oblong fingers or squares, wrap in waxed paper sprinkled liberally with sugar, then aluminium foil to stop humidity damaging the paste. Store in an airtight box or cool, dark cupboard.

BAKED QUINCES

COINGS AU FOUR

An autumn dessert that is irresistible in colour, texture and taste. Make sure you add the right amount of sugar to counteract the tartness of the fruit. Try muscovado if you can get it for the sprinkling sugar.

SERVES 4

4 VERY RIPE QUINCES, PEELED AND CORED
125 ml (4 fl oz) FULL CREAM
65 g (3 oz) FINE CASTOR SUGAR FOR THE STUFFING
130 g (5 oz) SUGAR FOR SPRINKLING

Place the quinces on a buttered baking dish.

Mix the cream with 60 g (2 oz) fine castor sugar and fill the cores of the quinces with this mixture. Sprinkle the fruit with a further 130 g (5 oz) of sugar. Place in a hot oven, 220°C (425°F; gas mark 7), for 30–35 minutes and baste several times as the fruit cooks.

PRESERVED LEMONS

CITRONS CONFITS

These days, with supermarkets supplying the same produce all year round, the seasonality of many fruits and vegetables has long been lost in the rush of modern living — along with, it is sad to say, a certain intensity of flavours that can only be appreciated fully when one lives by the seasons.

In earlier times, when lemons were precious and hard to come by, they were preserved in oil and used in ragouts and sautés. The advantage of this method is that you can use the whole of the lemon, without the skin tasting bitter. For variation, try adding 3–4 whole garlic cloves and some sprigs of thyme. Lemons preserved this way are ideal for adding to tagines or curries.

1 kg (2 lb 4 oz) UNTREATED LEMONS, WASHED AND WIPED
3 TABLESPOONS FINE SALT
SEVERAL WHOLE CLOVES GARLIC, PEELED (OPTIONAL)
12 SPRIGS THYME (OPTIONAL)
750–1000 ml (24–32 fl oz) OLIVE OIL

Cut the lemons into quarters lengthways and lay them down in a colander, skins facing up. Sprinkle with salt, cover with a linen tea towel and leave for about 12 hours.

The next day, drain the lemons and place in a large jar with a good airtight seal. Add the garlic and thyme if you wish. Pour in the olive oil, making sure it completely covers the lemons. Seal the jar and place it in a cool, dark place for at least a month before use. The lemons can then be used as and when you wish. The oil can be used separately in salad dressings.

CHESTNUT PRESERVE

CONFITURE DE MARRONS

A highly nutritious and energy-producing food, chestnuts were used as a basis for cooking in many parts of France in past centuries. The main area of production now is the Ardèche, but here in the Hérault, it is still possible to buy flour made from chestnuts, or bags of dried chestnuts which are great for soups and stews. In the late autumn, we can take a drive up the valley and collect baskets of them for making this delicate chestnut jam. Their uses are varied and many, both for sweet and savoury dishes, and if you cannot be bothered with all the peeling and shelling, try buying them canned.

MAKES APPROXIMATELY 8-10 POTS

2 kg (4 lb 8 oz) CHESTNUTS, PEELED
12 TABLESPOONS WATER
AN EQUAL QUANTITY OF SUGAR AS CHESTNUTS
2 VANILLA PODS, SPLIT

To peel the chestnuts: with a sharp knife, cut a nick in the shell of each nut and place them all in a baking tray with a little water in the bottom. Roast them in a very hot oven for about 10 minutes.

Take the chestnuts out of the oven and peel them while they are still hot.

Put the peeled chestnuts in a large pot, cover with cold water, bring to the boil and cook them for 40 minutes.

Drain off the water and rub them through a sieve or purée in a food processor. You may need to do this in several batches, because of the quantity.

Weigh the resulting purée, place in a jamming pan, and add an equal amount of sugar, the water and the vanilla pods. Heat the mixture slowly and stir continually.

The jam is ready when it comes away from the bottom of the pan as you stir it.

Turn off the heat, remove the vanilla pods and pot into sterilised jars.

WINTER

LEEK AND POTATO SOUP

CRÈME FLAMANDE

It sounds far too easy to be delicious, but this soup is very good. Taking just 5–10 minutes to prepare, and 20 minutes of cooking, it makes a hearty meal on its own, or a warming starter for a winter dinner party.

SERVES 4

2 LARGE LEEKS, CLEANED AND CHOPPED
1 LARGE ONION, PEELED AND SLICED
500 g (1 lb 2 oz) POTATOES, PEELED AND CUT INTO QUARTERS
SALT AND PEPPER
A KNOB OF BUTTER
1 LARGE ONION, PEELED AND DICED
100 ml (3 fl oz) CREAM
A FEW SPRIGS OF PARSLEY

Place the leeks, the sliced onion and the potatoes in a saucepan, and cover with 1 litre (2 pints) of water. Season with salt and pepper and bring to the boil, then simmer until the contents are quite soft. When cooked, blend the vegetables and the water they have cooked in to a purée.

In a smaller saucepan or frying pan melt a little butter and sweat the remaining onion. Do not let it brown — a low heat is best for this. When the onion is soft, add it to the purée. In the same smaller pan, heat the cream until it boils, and stir this into the soup. Adjust the seasoning if need be, transfer the hot soup to a warmed soup tureen, and garnish with a little chopped parsley.

COUNTRY ONION SOUP

SOUPE À L'OIGNON

A different version to the traditional baked onion soup that one usually comes across in France. This is equally heartening in the middle of a dark, cold winter. Always use mild onions as opposed to the strong yellow variety, and cook them well to prevent them from being indigestible.

SERVES 4

3 LARGE SWEET ONIONS, SLICED IN ROUNDS AS FINELY AS POSSIBLE
2 TABLESPOONS OLIVE OIL
SALT TO SEASON
1 LITRE (2 PINTS) COLD WATER OR STOCK
2 EGG YOLKS
A FEW DROPS VINEGAR
4 ROUNDS BAGUETTE, TOASTED

Heat the olive oil in a saucepan, and cook the sliced onions until they begin to soften. Season them with salt then cover the pan and leave to cook gently for 30 minutes. At this stage, they should be nicely pulpy-looking.

Pour over the cold water or stock and slowly bring to the boil, reduce the heat and simmer for 10 minutes.

Beat the egg yolks in a separate bowl with a few drops of vinegar and a little of the hot soup. Take the saucepan off the heat and add this mixture to it, stirring constantly. Return the saucepan to a very low heat and keep stirring until the mixture is hot again, but *do not* boil as the eggs will curdle.

Place a piece of toasted bread in each soup bowl (with a little grated gruyère cheese if you wish) and pour the soup over the bread. Garnish with freshly ground black pepper.

VEGETABLE SOUP

SOUPE À LA BONNE FEMME

A very old-fashioned recipe. Simple, quick and very cheap to make, it really is a good warming winter brew.

SERVES 4

35 g (1 oz) BUTTER
2 LARGE LEEKS, SLICED
3 CARROTS, DICED
500 g (1 lb 2 oz) POTATOES, DICED
1–2 TEASPOONS BROWN SUGAR
1 LITRE (2 PINTS) WATER OR STOCK
A LITTLE SALT
A LITTLE CREAM
PARSLEY OR CHERVIL WHEN AVAILABLE, TO GARNISH

In a saucepan, melt the butter and add the sliced leeks and diced carrots. Stir thoroughly and coat them with the butter. Add the potatoes and do the same. When the vegetables are heated through, add the sugar, then the stock or water and a little salt. Cook steadily for about 30 minutes without boiling.

If you like a creamed soup, pour the soup into a blender or food processor, and process until the mixture is smooth in consistency. If you prefer a chunky soup, leave it as it is.

When cooked, a little cream can be added if you wish. Garnish with some freshly chopped parsley or chervil.

PORK AND CABBAGE SOUP

POTÉE DE PORC DE BRETAGNE

Using the pot au feu principle of a whole meal cooked in one pot, this soup is a wonderfully hearty winter staple. You can drink the stock first like a soup, and then carve up the meats and sausages and have them as a second course with the vegetables.

SERVES 4

500 g (1 lb 2 oz) PICKLING PORK, WITHOUT BONE, OR MUTTON
400 g (14 oz) SMOKED PORK BELLY
1 MEDIUM HAM HOCK
BOUQUET GARNI
3 CARROTS, CUT IN HALF
1 SMALL SAVOY CABBAGE, CUT INTO 4
700 g (1 lb 9 oz) POTATOES, PEELED
500 g (1 lb 2 oz) PURE PORK SAUSAGES

Place the piece of pickling pork and the piece of smoked pork belly in a large stockpot and cover with cold water. Bring to the boil. Add the ham hock, bouquet garni and carrots, and leave to cook for 45 minutes on a good simmer.

Add the cabbage and let that cook for about 15 minutes, then add the potatoes and sausages and cook for another 30 minutes. Serve in large warmed bowls with a glass of cider.

TASTING PLATTER

ASSIETTE DE DÉGUSTATION

During the quieter months, we like to organise a dégustation (wine-tasting) schedule to help us keep up to date with all the new wines that are continually being released, and to discover new wine producers that we have not come across before. Often when you arrive at a *caveau* for a tasting they will have a small basket of walnuts or perhaps some saucisson sliced in rounds for you to nibble on while you are tasting. The idea is to refresh the palate and encourage the saliva glands. Some people prefer to nibble on a simple slice of rye or white bread now and then, or to sip some water, but whatever you choose for your tasting platter it is important to think about the types of wines you are serving and adjust the ingredients to suit.

In our region, which is best known for its red wines, I always include a strong blue cheese as the main focus. That would probably be the strongest flavour on the platter. To that I would add some fresh green olives, brine cured rather than vinegar based, which are quite fruity, and some nutty rye bread, sliced finely. A good firm pure pork saucisson is invaluable, not too dry and preferably without peppercorns. And a mild goat or sheep cheese is also excellent with red wine.

For a less serious tasting platter, where you are choosing the platter as an hors d'oeuvre as opposed to a palate refresher, the scope is broader. Numerous pâtés and spreads like Brandade de Morue (page 13), and Fricandeau (page 72) can be included, or Anchoïade (page 36) with *crudités* — the emphasis is then more on the food accompanied by wine, rather than the reverse.

PAN-FRIED FATTENED-DUCK LIVER

FOIE GRAS POÊLÉ

It may seem rather strange that we have included this recipe, when it is virtually impossible to obtain raw foie gras anywhere outside of France. The simple fact is that this dish is so typically French, and so sublime when one is fortunate enough to experience it, that it is worth including for those two reasons alone. For the true Francophile, any visit to France will provide an opportunity to try this gastronomic delicacy, and perhaps you will be able to purchase a fattened duck or goose liver in one of the specialist markets that sell them, and have a go at cooking it for yourself.

Some things to look out for. It is very expensive, and more so just prior to Christmas, so only the freshest, finest quality putty-coloured duck or goose livers should be used for this dish. The pan must be seeringly hot so that the slices of liver cook very fast, but do not melt completely. Despite the very fine and delicate flavour of foie gras it is dangerously rich, so two slices per person are more than ample. The temptation is to have more, but speaking from experience, your night will be far more tranquil if you practise a little restraint.

A RAW (*CRU*) DUCK OR GOOSE LIVER, 500–700 g
(1–1lb 8 oz), THE FRESHEST POSSIBLE
A LITTLE SALT

Take a large frying pan and wipe it very clean with a paper towel and some fine salt.

Wash the whole liver carefully under cold water, rather like you would a newborn baby, but without the soap. Place it on a linen towel and carefully pat it dry. Remove any tubes, threads or loose skin from the liver with the point of a thin-bladed knife.

With a sharp knife, slice the liver into pieces about 2.5 cm (1 inch) thick. It will feel rather like cutting into butter.

Heat the frying pan to very, very hot and carefully

TOP: THE MARCHE AU GRAS AT CASTRES — CHOOSING FOIE GRAS TO PRESERVE AND COOK À LA POÊLE

BOTTOM: FATTENED-DUCK LIVERS PRESERVED IN THEIR OWN FAT. CONSIDERED TO BE ONE OF FRANCE'S GREATEST DELICACIES, FOIE GRAS IS EATEN ON SPECIAL OCCASIONS.

place the slices, one by one, into the pan. They should only need a minute or two on each side, until they brown rather like a rare steak. Remove from the pan and quickly drain on a paper towel. Season with some fine salt and serve as hot as possible with a plainly dressed spinach salad and a glass of muscat or sauterne.

ANCHOVIES IN PUFF PASTRY

AMUSE-GUEULE AUX ANCHOIS

When serving hors d'oeuvres with drinks, it is often a good idea to include something with a salty flavour, as the salt stimulates the gastric juices. Anchovies cooked lightly in puff pastry somehow lose a little of their strong salty flavour but remain tangy enough to satisfy roaming tastebuds at apéritif time.

A variation of this recipe is to replace the anchovies with a dob of Brandade de Morue (see page 13).

MAKES 24

125 g (4 oz) PUFF PASTRY
24 ANCHOVY FILLETS, PRESERVED IN OIL
BEATEN EGG YOLK TO DRESS THE PASTRY

Roll out the pastry into a square, 5 mm ($\frac{1}{4}$ inch) thick. Cut the pastry square into 24 narrow strips about twice the length of an anchovy fillet.

Place each of the anchovy fillets at one end of a pastry strip and roll up into a pinwheel shape. Place on a lightly greased oven tray and brush with beaten egg.

Place the tray in the oven, preheated to 230°C (450°F; gas mark 8). Cook for about 10 minutes, or until the pastry is light and golden. Serve warm or cold with apéritifs.

SARDINE PÂTÉ

PÂTÉ DE SARDINES

Ideal for a tasty lunch on a busy day, or for hors d'oeuvres, this is a recipe to adapt to your own taste. We like to include chilli powder or Harissa (see page 125) to give it a bit of bite, and we make it with a fairly coarse texture. You may prefer it smooth and without chilli — something to experiment with.

SERVES 2

125 g (4 oz) TINNED SARDINES IN OIL
1 ONION, STRONG OR MILD TO TASTE, DICED
1 TABLESPOON VINEGAR
1 TEASPOON HARISSA OR PINCH OF CHILLI POWDER, TO TASTE

Empty the sardines into a bowl and crumble with a fork to give the desired texture.

Add the onion, harissa or chilli powder, and vinegar. Mix well.

Serve with toasted rye bread or salty crackers, and a bowl of green olives.

HERRINGS WITH POTATOES AND GHERKINS

HARENGS AUX POMMES DE TERRE ET AUX CORNICHONS

Dropping in on our bachelor friend, Jean-Jacques, just before midday was a good move, because as a result we got to try this typically peasant dish from the Languedoc region, and then got shown how to make it. To Jean-Jacques it was a staple, something he could produce without thinking, but with the obvious virtues of being cheap to make, filling and delicious. He would be the first to say that there is no recipe — more an idea, somewhere to start and to adapt to suit your own tastes. But that is a fundamental principle for developing your own style of cooking.

SERVES 4

225 g (8 oz) SMOKED HERRING FILLETS IN OIL, CUT INTO
SMALL PIECES, 1 cm (1/2 inch) LONG
450 g (1 lb) POTATOES, PEELED AND QUARTERED
1 SMALL MILD ONION, DICED COARSELY
2–3 LARGE GHERKINS, SLICED
PINCH OF CHILLI POWDER, TO TASTE
2–3 TABLESPOONS OLIVE OIL
GROUND BLACK PEPPER AND SEA SALT, TO TASTE

Boil the potatoes in salted water, cooking them until soft, 15–20 minutes. Strain and allow to cool.

Place the herring pieces, potatoes, onion, gherkins, chilli powder and olive oil in a bowl. Mix the ingredients together carefully so that the potatoes do not break up. Grind over the black pepper and sea salt, and serve.

SALAD OF BELGIAN ENDIVE

SALADE D'ENDIVES

A delicious winter salad which can be served as a first course or as an interlude between courses. The recipe was given to us by a Biterrois (someone from Béziers, our nearest large town) friend who was generous enough to pass on his family's recipe. The first time we ate it was actually in springtime at his sister's house, after we had been to the market to buy all the ingredients fresh that morning.

SERVES 4

2 TABLESPOONS OLIVE OIL
2 TEASPOONS RED-WINE VINEGAR
1/2 TEASPOON ANCHOVY PASTE OR 2 TEASPOONS
ANCHOVY OIL
4 ENDIVES, WASHED AND DRIED
A HANDFUL OF BLACK OLIVES
SALT AND PEPPER

Make the vinaigrette in the bottom of the bowl in which you will serve the salad. Whisk together the oil and vinegar, then add the anchovy paste or anchovy oil.

With a sharp knife, cut the core from the root end of each endive. Discard any browned outside leaves and cut the endives in halves and quarters, so you have leaves of a manageable size. Put the leaves into the dressing.

Slice slivers of black olive off the stone onto the endives. Add some freshly ground sea salt and black pepper, toss and leave for 30 minutes before serving with fresh baguette or brown bread.

ONION TART

TARTE À L'OIGNON

This tasty tart makes a delicious entrée all year round, but especially in winter with a dandelion salad to follow. The taste of the tart will actually vary depending on the time of year you cook it and the onions used. In the summer months, when onions are sweeter, it is milder in flavour. As a variation, try Spanish red onions for colour.

SERVES 6

250 g (9 oz) PÂTE BRISÉE (SEE PAGE 121)
50 g (2 oz) BUTTER OR 2 TABLESPOONS OIL
700 g (1 lb 9 oz) SWEET ONIONS, PEELED AND SLICED
FINELY
NUTMEG, FRESHLY MILLED PEPPER AND SEA SALT
TO SEASON
3 EGG YOLKS
125 ml (4 fl oz) CREAM

Make the pastry and leave to stand in the refrigerator for at least 30 minutes.

In the meantime, heat some butter or oil in a heavy-based frying pan, and cook the onions slowly without frying them. Stir from time to time so that they do not stick to the bottom of the pan. This will take 20–30 minutes. Season with freshly ground pepper, salt and some freshly grated nutmeg.

Take the pan off the heat and allow it to cool. Stir in the well-beaten egg yolks and the cream.

Oil a 25-cm (10-inch) tart tin, and roll out the pastry fairly thinly. Line the tin with pastry and trim the edges. Pour the filling onto the pastry, and spread the mixture evenly. Bake in a hot oven, 200°C (400°F; gas mark 6), for 30 minutes. Serve very hot.

CHICKEN IN MUSTARD

POULET À LA MOUTARDE

This is a French classic from the Bourgogne which never fails to please. Somehow the mustard in the cooking process loses its sting, to provide the base for the wonderful tasty sauce. With the plump chicken falling off the bone, it all melts in the mouth.

SERVES 4

1–1.5 kg (2–3 lb 8 oz) FARM-RAISED CHICKEN
1 TABLESPOON VEGETABLE OIL
2 CLOVES GARLIC, PEELED
GROUND BLACK PEPPER AND SALT, TO TASTE
2–4 TABLESPOONS DIJON MUSTARD
200 ml (7 fl oz) CREAM

Put the chicken in a roasting pan with a little oil. Place the garlic cloves in the cavity. Season with pepper and salt. Coat all of the exterior of the chicken liberally with the mustard. Cover with cooking foil.

Preheat the oven to 180°C (350°F; gas mark 4). Roast the chicken for 55 minutes per kg (25 minutes per pound), removing the foil for the final 10 minutes.

When cooked, scrape the mustard off the chicken into the pan. Place the chicken on a serving dish. Add the cream to the mustard and cooking juices in the pan and simmer for 5 minutes, stirring occasionally. Pour the sauce into a jug. Carve the chicken and serve dressed with the mustard sauce.

CHICKEN AND LEEK PIE

TOURTE DE POULET AUX POIREAUX

A pie as such is rather an old-fashioned phenomenon these days. They are a rustic, regional alternative to fine-dining tarts and pastry concoctions in France. This does not make them any less delicious, just hard to find. The basic difference between a tart and a torte, according to Larousse, is that a tart does not have a pastry lid whereas a torte generally does. They can be sweet or savoury.

<u>SERVES 4–6</u>

APPROXIMATELY 500 g (1 lb 2 oz) PÂTE BRISÉE
(SEE PAGE 121)
6 MEDIUM-SIZED CHICKEN BREASTS
2–3 TABLESPOONS OLIVE OIL OR BUTTER
3–4 LEEKS, TRIMMED, WASHED WELL AND CUT INTO
ROUNDS
2 CLOVES GARLIC, CRUSHED
SEVERAL SPRIGS FRESH THYME OR SAGE
30 g (1 oz) UNSALTED BUTTER
25 g (1 oz) FLOUR
500 ml (1 pint) CHICKEN STOCK
SALT AND PEPPER TO SEASON
A LITTLE MILK OR EGG YOLK TO BRUSH THE PASTRY

Make the pastry in advance and leave it in the refrigerator to rest.

In a large frying pan, brown the breasts of chicken lightly in the olive oil. Remove from the pan and put to one side to cool. Alternatively, you can poach the chicken breasts in chicken stock (5–10 minutes only). I prefer to sauté them as I like the look and taste of the meat lightly golden, but the preference is purely personal.

Add the leeks to the pan and sauté, adding the crushed garlic and the fresh thyme with the stalks removed. When the leeks are nicely golden and soft, remove them and put them with the chicken.

Make a béchamel sauce by melting the unsalted butter in a saucepan then adding the flour to make a roux. Cook the roux on a medium heat for about 4 minutes then reduce to a very low heat. Add the chicken stock little by little, stirring vigorously so that any lumps

that form are beaten out. It is often easier to do this with a whisk than a wooden spoon. Season with salt and pepper and when the sauce is nicely thickened and coats the back of a wooden spoon, turn off the heat.

Divide the pastry in half and roll out on a floured surface. Roll out the bottom first — this should be sufficiently large to cover a 20-cm (8-inch) round pie dish. Roll out the top marginally larger, and have it at the ready.

Cut the chicken breasts into thick strips and place them on top of the pastry base. Next add the leek mixture with its juices, so that it is spread evenly among the chicken. Finally pour over the thick béchamel sauce so that there is enough to partially cover the contents of the pie, but not so much that it will overflow when cooking in the oven.

Close the pie with the pastry lid, trim and knit the edges together, pressing a fork all around the edge of the pastry. Make several slits in the top for the steam to escape, and decorate if you want with any leftover strips of pastry. Brush with a beaten egg and place in a hot oven, 200°C (400°F; gas mark 6), for 30 minutes, or until the pastry is nicely golden. Serve hot.

ROASTED GOOSE WITH CHESTNUT AND SAGE STUFFING

OIE ROTIE FARCIE AUX MARRONS ET À LA SAUGE

Like everywhere else in the world, the French have certain traditional dishes that they like to eat at Christmas time. Preferences vary from region to region, and the meal is often a six- or eight-course affair. Foie gras usually features somewhere around the beginning, and after the second or third courses the main dish will arrive, more often than not being a turkey, chapon or goose with chestnut stuffing. If you make it through to the fifth and sixth courses you will be looking at either a Bûche de Noël or Christmas Yule log made from sponge cake, chestnut purée and chocolate. Or if you happen to be in the south-east, it is likely that you will be presented with the 13 little desserts of Christmas, representing the 13 participants at the Last Supper, which are made up of various sweetmeats, dried fruits and pastries. Wherever you are, it is a feast and one that usually takes several days and a few long walks to get over.

SERVES 6–8

1 x 5 kg (11 lb) OVEN-READY GOOSE

FOR THE STUFFING

900 g (2 lb) CHESTNUTS (CANNED ARE FINE)
30 g (1 oz) BUTTER
2 SHALLOTS, CHOPPED FINELY
LIVER, GIBLETS AND HEART FROM THE GOOSE, CHOPPED
200 g (7 oz) MINCED VEAL
500 g (1 lb 2 oz) SWEET APPLES, STEWED IN A LITTLE WATER
6 SAGE LEAVES, CHOPPED
SALT AND PEPPER

Drain the chestnuts and place them in a bowl, crumbling them a little with your hands.

Melt the butter in a frying pan, and sauté the shallots, goose liver, giblets and heart. Add the minced veal and cook for a few minutes more. Add this mixture to the chestnuts, then the stewed apples and chopped sage, and season with salt and pepper. Stir well so that all the ingredients are combined.

Prick the skin of the goose all over with a metal skewer, place it in a basin and pour over about 2 litres (3¹/₂ pints) of boiling water. This is to help the fat run off the bird while it is cooking. Wipe the surface of the goose dry with paper towels.

Spoon the stuffing into the cavity of the bird, and close the aperture with thread or a small metal skewer; even a couple of metal safety pins will work wonders. Massage the skin of the goose with plenty of fine salt, at least 2 tablespoons for a bird of this size. Place the bird on a metal roasting rack or cake rack in a spacious roasting pan.

Place in a moderate oven, 190°C (375°F; gas mark 5), for 3–3¹/₂ hours. After the first hour or so, pour off the liquid goose fat into a container and reserve. It will keep well in the refrigerator, and is delicious for cooking potatoes.

When the goose is cooked, serve with a sauce made by deglazing the meat juices in the roasting pan with cognac or white wine and boiling over a high heat for a few minutes, accompanied by your favourite Christmas vegetables.

JUGGED RABBIT

CIVET DE LAPIN

In past times when this region was very poor, few people could afford meat as daily sustenance. There was not a lavish supply of beef, lamb, pork and poultry as there is now; instead they kept goats, shot what game they could when it was available, and raised rabbits. That is how this dish came to be a hearty working-man's staple.

Many people in our small village kept their own rabbits, gathering grains and grasses on their way home from the fields to feed their animals. In the latter part of last century myxomatosis wiped out the local rabbit population and the introduction of vineyards and wine-making provided wealth so that people were able to afford other kinds of meat and poultry.

Today, old Monsieur and Madame Torres are the only couple in our village who still raise their own rabbits, and these are delicious. Fed on a diet of corn and lucerne, the meat is lean, tender and full of flavour. We can order our rabbits a day in advance (freshly butchered meat must always be left to rest for 24 hours) and the following day the carefully prepared rabbits are ready and waiting. The blood is put aside in a jar mixed with some red-wine vinegar for the sauce. Without this vital ingredient, a Civet de Lapin would not be a civet but simply a rabbit casserole.

SERVES 4–6

1–2 SKINNED AND CLEANED RABBITS, CUT INTO PIECES
THE BLOOD OF THE RABBIT TOGETHER WITH ABOUT
100 ml (3 fl oz) RED-WINE VINEGAR
2–3 TABLESPOONS OLIVE OIL
1 1/2 MEDIUM ONIONS, GRATED
3 SHALLOTS, GRATED
1/2 ONION AND 1 SHALLOT, CHOPPED UP COARSELY
WITH THE RABBIT LIVER
250 g (9 oz) LARDONS OR CHOPPED STREAKY BACON
1–2 TABLESPOONS WHITE FLOUR
ABOUT 600 ml (20 fl oz) GOOD FULL-BODIED RED WINE
BOUQUET GARNI OF THYME, BAY AND PARSLEY
COARSE-GRAIN SEA SALT AND FRESHLY GROUND PEPPER

Pour about 2–3 tablespoons of olive oil into a heavy-based frying pan and heat to a reasonably high temperature. Add the pieces of rabbit one by one, and brown on both sides. Put these to one side in a deep cast-iron casserole. Add the onions, shallots, livers and lardons to the frying pan, reducing the heat slightly if necessary, and stir so that they do not stick.

Once nicely browned, transfer to the casserole now placed on the top of the stove on a moderate heat. Sprinkle the flour over the meat and gently stir it in. Quickly pour over the red wine until the meat is practically covered. The amount of wine you use will depend on the size of the rabbit. Add the bouquet garni, the jar of blood and red-wine vinegar, and season with salt and ground pepper.

Raise the heat again slightly and simmer until the sauce reduces and the rabbit is tender. Again, this will depend on the size of the rabbit, but for a medium-sized rabbit cooking steadily, allow around 1–1 1/2 hours.

When the rabbit is cooked, place the meat in an ovenproof dish and keep warm. Turn the heat up high on the remaining sauce to reduce it slightly if you find there is still too much liquid. Remove the bouquet garni and press the sauce through a sieve or mouli. This will give your sauce a smoother, more creamy texture. Return the sauce to the heat and add the pieces of rabbit, letting it simmer for a further 5 minutes. Serve piping hot with a steaming bowl of boiled potatoes.

SMOKED SALMON WITH NOODLES

NOUILLES AU SAUMON FUMÉ

In the south of France, a wide range of fresh and dried pastas are consumed daily. The habit is surprisingly ancient, dating back to the time of the famous Catherine de Médici, who brought pasta from Italy to France. Its uses are as varied in French cooking as they are in Italian, from the famous Provençal classics like Pâtés au Pistou and Soupe au Pistou, to plain buttered or oiled noodles, served with a Daube of Beef.

The following dish, though rich, is also very light and can be served as an entrée or main course. The salmon can be replaced with any other smoked or poached fish or shellfish, like oysters, mussels or paua/abalone. Whatever fish or shellfish you use, make sure it is in bite-sized pieces, and take care not to over-handle it. Make sure you adjust the herbs according to the type of fish you use.

SERVES 4

250 g (9 oz) PASTA NOODLES (TAGLIATELLE OR
FETTUCCINE IS BEST)
2–3 TABLESPOONS OLIVE OIL
3–4 MEDIUM-SIZED LEEKS, CHOPPED
1 LARGE CLOVE GARLIC, CRUSHED
2–3 SPRIGS FRESH LEMON THYME (TRY TARRAGON WITH
OYSTERS, FINELY SHREDDED SPINACH OR FLAT-LEAFED
PARSLEY WITH PAUA/ABALONE)
A GENEROUS HANDFUL TOASTED PINE NUTS
JUICE OF 1 MEDIUM-SIZED LEMON
GROUND BLACK PEPPER, LOTS
450 g (1 lb) CRÈME FRAÎCHE
250 g (9 oz) SMOKED SALMON, CUT INTO WIDE STRIPS.

Boil a generous-sized pan of water for the noodles with a tablespoon of olive oil and a teaspoon of salt. Add the noodles and cook quickly until al dente (fresh noodles should only need about 4 minutes). Drain.

Heat the olive oil in a heavy-based frying pan and sauté the chopped leeks and garlic. When they are opaque and lightly golden add the lemon thyme, taking care to remove the stalks. Toss in the pine nuts and add the lemon juice, and stir. Grind over some black pepper and spoon in the crème fraîche. Mix well.

Finally add the smoked salmon to the sauce in the frying pan. Cook gently for about 1 minute (do not overcook). Add the noodles and combine all the ingredients well.

Serve garnished with your favourite herb or chopped parsley and some freshly ground sea salt.

NOTE: Parmesan cheese is not an ideal accompaniment for this dish as you will lose all the subtle flavours of the fish.

BELOW: A CROWDED FISH COUNTER AT LES HALLES, THE MAIN PRODUCE MARKET IN BEZIÉRS.

TURKEY CURRY

CURRY DE DINDE

It is only after being in France for a short time that one realises there is nothing highly spiced in native French cuisine. All the spiced food that one finds here comes from abroad, from France's latter-day colonies in North Africa and the East. There is the occasional Chinese or Vietnamese restaurant but not the proliferation that is found in other countries. If you want tasty, spicy, hot food, then you really need to go to Paris, or make it yourself. And we frequently do for ourselves, and for our guests once we have got to know them a little.

SERVES 4–6

600 g (1 lb 5 oz) TURKEY BREASTS, SLICED INTO PORTIONS
2 TABLESPOONS VEGETABLE OIL
1 LARGE ONION, SLICED
1–2 CLOVES GARLIC, CRUSHED
2 TABLESPOONS CURRY POWDER OR PASTE
500 g (1 lb 2 oz) TOMATO PURÉE
1 CUP WATER
SALT, TO TASTE
1–2 TEASPOONS FRESH CORIANDER, CHOPPED

In a frying pan or cocotte, heat the oil to a medium heat, add the onion and garlic, and sauté until they start to brown. Add the curry powder or paste and allow to cook for 3–4 minutes, stirring. Add the turkey breasts and sauté on both sides to seal in the juices.

Add the tomato purée and a cup of water. Season with salt, stir and reduce the heat to a simmer. Cook gently until the turkey is tender (30–40 minutes), stirring occasionally. Serve on rice, with chopped coriander as a garnish.

TUNA CURRY

CURRY DE THON

SERVES 4

150 g (5 oz) TINNED TUNA IN OIL
1 LARGE ONION, SLICED
2 TABLESPOONS VEGETABLE OIL
2–3 CLOVES GARLIC, CRUSHED
2 TABLESPOONS CURRY POWDER OR PASTE
500 g (1 lb 2 oz) TOMATO PURÉE
90 g (3 oz) SULTANAS
1–2 TEASPOONS LEMON PEEL, FINELY SLICED
1–2 TABLESPOONS LEMON JUICE
250 ml (9 fl oz) WATER

FOR THE SALAD

1 FRESH TOMATO, SLICED
2 TABLESPOONS VINEGAR

To make the salad, put a quarter of the sliced onion in a bowl with the tomato, dress with the vinegar and set aside for the salad garnish.

Heat the oil in a frying pan or cocotte to a medium heat, add the rest of the onion and the garlic, and sauté until they start to brown. Add the curry powder or paste and allow to cook for 3–4 minutes.

Add the tuna, tomato purée, sultanas, lemon peel, lemon juice and water, and stir. Cook gently for 15 minutes, covered, and then 15–20 minutes uncovered, to allow the sauce to reduce. Serve on rice, garnished with the onion and tomato salad.

BEAN CASSEROLE WITH PRESERVED MEATS

CASSOULET

There are officially three major versions of cassoulet, which originate from Toulouse, Carcassonne and Castelnaudary in the south-west of France. The three versions vary in their cooking methods and ingredients, but the basics remain constant — dried white haricot beans, a good quality pork sausage, some pork spare-rib and one other meat, either a breast or shoulder of lamb or mutton, or portions of preserved duck or goose, and a good hearty appetite!

Cassoulet is essentially a family dish, preferably eaten at midday, and preferably on a holiday or Sunday. If you are going to serve anything else with the cassoulet, as anyone who has ever eaten a cassoulet will know, a plain green salad served either before or after it will certainly surface. It is a serious eating experience!

SERVES 6

500 g (1 lb 2 oz) DRIED WHITE HARICOT BEANS
1 HEAPED TEASPOON SALT
BOUQUET GARNI OF BAY, FRESH THYME AND PARSLEY
1 ONION, PEELED AND PRICKED WITH 2 CLOVES
1 FRESH TOMATO, CUT INTO QUARTERS AND SEEDED
1 kg (2 lb 4 oz) SHOULDER OF LAMB OR MUTTON, CUT
INTO PIECES
OR
A DUCK PARTLY ROASTED AND THEN JOINTED (INSTEAD
OF PRESERVED DUCK OR GOOSE PORTIONS)
125 g (4 oz) FATTY BACON OR SALT PORK, IN THICK SLICES
OF ABOUT 2–3 cm (1 inch)
250 g (9 oz) FRESH PURE PORK OR GARLIC SAUSAGE
3 CLOVES GARLIC
SMALL QUANTITY OF BREADCRUMBS

Put the dried beans into a little cold water, and rub them between your hands to get any dust off them. Drain off that water and change the water twice more, rinsing the beans thoroughly. When the water runs clear, you will know that the beans are clean enough for the next stage.

Put the beans in a stockpot with 2 litres (4 pints) of cold water. Bring to the boil, cover, remove from the heat and leave them for 40 minutes. The beans will swell, go white and emit the oxide of potassium which normally makes them indigestible. The other method of doing this is to soak the beans in cold water overnight. Do not skip this step — it is essential; if you miss it, your cassoulet will be inedible.

Discard the water again. Return the beans to the rinsed pot and add about 1.5 litres (3 pints) of tepid water, a heaped teaspoon of salt, the bouquet garni, the onion stuck with cloves, and the tomato. Bring to the boil, then reduce to a steady simmer, and cook gently for about $1^1/_2$ hours, until the beans are about half cooked.

In the meantime, partly roast the duck, and in a frying pan slowly brown the pieces of bacon or salt pork, and the sausage cut up into pieces about the length of your index finger.

When the beans are ready, do not discard the liquid this time, but spoon half the beans into a spacious, round casserole dish. On top of the beans, arrange the sausages, mutton or lamb pieces, and the duck pieces. To that add the garlic cloves then cover with the rest of the beans and their liquid. Place in a slow to medium oven, 160°C (325°F; gas mark 3), for another $1^1/_2$ hours.

About 15 minutes before serving sprinkle the top with home-made breadcrumbs, and grill gently so that a light crust forms on the top. When ready the cassoulet should still be moist and the beans soft but well formed, not mushy.

Serve piping hot on warmed plates, making sure that everyone gets a piece of each type of meat and the beans to accompany it. A light Côte du Rhone-style red wine is ideal for drinking with a good cassoulet. And afterwards, a long walk is recommended.

SPIT-ROASTED LEG OF LAMB

GIGOT À LA FLAMBADOU

A flambadou is an instrument which looks like a giant-sized candle-snuffer. The snuffer part is a hollow cone made of steel plate, with a hole at the small end, and there is a handle that is usually about a metre long. The idea is that once the leg of lamb, or gigot, is ready you take the flambadou, which has been heated to red-heat in the barbecue, and hold it over the gigot, which is still turning on the spit. You introduce a piece of pork lard into the snuffer. The lard melts and produces a stream of liquid fat which bastes the gigot. The stream of fat often ignites and produces a spectacular display of molten fire. The spectacle lasts only a few minutes, but the taste added to the meat is . . . *magnifique!*

SERVES 6–8

1–1.5 kg (2 lb 4 oz–3 lb 6 oz) LEG OF LAMB
SALT
VEGETABLE OIL
125 g (4 oz) PURE PORK FAT

Massage a little oil and salt into the leg of lamb. This will crisp the skin.

The simplest and quickest method is to roast the leg of lamb in the oven, 40–60 minutes per kg (2 lb 4 oz) at 180°C (350°F; gas mark 4). When the meat is almost cooked, mount the leg on the turnspit, and finish it off over the barbecue. When just cooked, finish by basting, using the flambadou.

BAKED GARLIC PURÉE

PURÉE D'AIL AU FOUR

As an alternative to straight baked garlic, served as an accompaniment to grilled and roasted meats, this variation makes a nice change from fiddling about with garlic skins on your plate. Serve the purée in a ramekin next to the meat on the main plate or just spoon a knob of it onto a tasty char-grilled steak. The purée is also an ideal condiment for making soups and sauces.

SERVES 6–8

3–4 WHOLE CORMS GARLIC, CLEANED AND TRIMMED
3–4 TABLESPOONS OLIVE OIL
SEVERAL PINCHES FRESHLY GROUND SEA SALT

Arrange the well-trimmed garlic in a baking dish. Drizzle over the olive oil and sprinkle the ground sea salt on top. Place in a medium oven, 180°C (350°F; gas mark 4), and bake until the garlic bulbs are soft and nicely browned — about 30-40 minutes usually.

Remove from the oven and allow to cool slightly. Squeeze the bulbs of cooked garlic from their skins, and either pass through a sieve or mash roughly with a fork.

Turn out into a small serving dish or spoon directly onto any grilled meat.

BEEF IN RED WINE

DAUBE DE BOEUF PROVENÇALE

A daube could be described as a stew made with wine. But of course there is more to it than that. Daubes are a peasant dish traditional to southern France. They are made with the cheaper, tougher cuts of meat, like shin or neck, which after hours of gentle cooking become tender and full of taste. The traditional method of making a daube is that all the ingredients are placed in a cocotte (cast-iron casserole), which would be placed on the embers of the cooking fire just before the vineyard workers left for a day in the vines. The daube would simmer away slowly all day, gradually tenderising the meat, to be ready to satisfy the most demanding hunger when the workers return.

I first cooked a daube from an Elizabeth David recipe. Not having unsmoked bacon, I used smoked streaky bacon instead. This transferred a certain smokiness to the dish, which I liked, and which has become part of how I cook the dish now.

My first experience of flaming off the alcohol from the wine made me think that I was a real cook at last. This step is not included in all daube recipes, but it certainly adds to the final result.

SERVES 6

900 g (2 lb) BEEF SHIN, NECK OR SHOULDER
170 g (6 oz) SMOKED STREAKY BACON, DICED
2 TABLESPOONS OLIVE OIL
2 MEDIUM-SIZED ONIONS, SLICED
2–4 CARROTS, SLICED
2 TOMATOES, SLICED
ORANGE ZEST
2 CLOVES GARLIC, CHOPPED COARSELY
BOUQUET GARNI OF THYME, BAY AND PARSLEY
1 GLASS GOOD RED WINE
GROUND PEPPER AND SALT, TO TASTE

Cut the meat into slices about 2.5 cm (1 inch) thick and 3–5 cm (1–2 inches) square.

To the cocotte, add the olive oil, onions, carrots, tomatoes, bacon, orange zest and garlic, then add the meat in layers, burying the bouquet garni in the middle.

Heat the cocotte, uncovered, on the stove on a medium heat for 10 minutes.

While this is happening, pour the wine into a saucepan, bring it to a fast boil, light the vapours with a match and continue to swirl the pan to flame off the alcohol.

Add the wine to the cocotte. Cover with the lid, and place in a very low oven, 130°C (260°F; gas mark 1), to cook slowly for 3–5 hours, until the meat is tender. Serve with boiled potatoes, Caramelised Turnips (see page 111) or buttered noodles.

NOTE: This recipe is also superb cooked with wild boar, if you can get hold of some.

STUFFED LEG OF LAMB IN PASTRY

GIGOT D'AGNEAU EN CROÛTE

Cooking a small leg of lamb this way allows the meat to retain its moisture. It cooks more quickly and the flavours are retained within the parcel in rather the same fashion as cooking fish en papiotte. The same principle can be employed for cooking rabbit.

SERVES 4–6

1 kg (2 lb 4 oz) LEG OF LAMB, BONED
250 g (9 oz) TAPENADE (SEE PAGE 37)
2 TABLESPOONS OLIVE OIL
SALT AND PEPPER
230 g (8 oz) PUFF PASTRY
1 EGG YOLK, BEATEN

Make the tapenade in advance.

Fill the cavity where the bone has been removed from the leg of lamb with tapenade, and close the opening with a few stitches of string. Massage the olive oil into the skin of the lamb with your fingers. Season with salt and pepper.

Place the lamb in a roasting pan, in a very hot oven, 240°C (475°F; gas mark 9), for 15 minutes to seal the meat and its juices.

Roll out the puff pastry on a floured surface, so that it is large enough to wrap over the leg of lamb. Remove the lamb from the oven and wrap the pastry neatly around the leg, brush with the beaten egg yolk and return to the oven for 20–25 minutes to finish cooking. If you prefer your lamb less pink, leave it longer. Serve with Ratatouille (see page 58) and roasted potatoes.

GREEN LENTILS WITH SALTED PORK

LENTILLES AU PETIT SALÉ

You could not find more traditional winter fare than this in France. Be it on the menu of some Parisian bistro or bubbling away on the hearth in a Languedocien wine-grower's house, this hearty dish is guaranteed to keep out the coldest winter chills. The best green lentils come from the Puy de Dôme in central France and are usually marked so on the packet. All lentils have an extremely high nutritional value, being rich in protein, carbo-hydrates, B vitamins and iron.

The pork referred to in this dish is the breast, belly or flank of salt pork that we Anglo-Saxons would normally use for pickling. It is cut into pieces at the end of cooking. If you are in doubt about the cut required, check with your butcher. If that is too hard, use diced pieces of salt pork.

SERVES 4

500 g (1 lb 2 oz) GREEN LENTILS, WASHED AND DRAINED
1 MEDIUM-SIZED ONION, CHOPPED FINELY
2 CARROTS, CHOPPED FINELY
BOUQUET GARNI (1 BAY LEAF, SPRIGS OF FRESH THYME
AND PARSLEY TIED TOGETHER)
8 PEPPERCORNS
SPRIG OF FRESH SAGE
300 g (10 oz) SALT PORK BREAST, BELLY OR FLANK
6 SMOKED PORK SAUSAGES
4 TABLESPOONS OLIVE OIL

Put the washed lentils, finely chopped onion and carrots, the bouquet garni, peppercorns and sage into a large saucepan. Cover with cold water and bring to the boil. As soon as the liquid begins to boil, reduce the heat to a slow simmer. Add the salt pork, smoked sausages and olive oil. Cover and leave to cook for 35–40 minutes.

When the lentils are cooked (you want them slightly al dente like a good pasta) discard the bouquet garni, drain what liquid remains, and turn out onto a warmed serving dish. Cut the salt pork into pieces and arrange on top of the lentils or around the edges along with the smoked sausages.

NOTE: The secret with the seasoning for this dish is to check halfway through the cooking, and to adjust by adding a little more salt, if necessary.

RAGOUT OF RED KIDNEY BEANS AND LEEKS

RAGOÛT DE HARICOTS ROUGES ET DE POIREAUX

This ragout is Corsican in origin. It is rich in protein and vitamins, and guaranteed to satisfy the heartiest of appetites. Either canned or dried red kidney beans can be used. If the latter are used, they must be soaked in cold water overnight and cooked for 30 minutes prior to using.

SERVES 4

500 g (1 lb 2 oz) RED KIDNEY BEANS, CANNED OR DRIED
3 LARGE LEEKS, WASHED, TRIMMED AND CUT INTO ROUNDS
1 TABLESPOON DUCK FAT OR OLIVE OIL
1 OR 2 SAUSAGES PER PERSON, PREFERABLY PURE PORK OR VENISON, WITH NO BREADCRUMBS
OR
500 g (1 lb 2 oz) SALTED PORK BELLY, GRILLED THEN CUT INTO CHUNKS
1 GOOD SPRIG FRESH THYME
400 g (14 oz) TOMATO PURÉE
200 ml (7 fl oz) WATER
1 CLOVE GARLIC, FLATTENED UNDER THE BLADE OF A KNIFE

If using dried red kidney beans, soak them overnight. In the morning, drain and place them in a saucepan. Add enough fresh cold water so that they are just covered. Bring to the boil and cook for 30 minutes. Drain.

Heat the duck fat in a heavy-based casserole dish. Toss in the chopped leeks and brown them slightly over a medium heat. Add the sausages or pork belly, and brown. Sprinkle over the fresh thyme, add the beans and pour in the tomato purée and water. Stir well, add the garlic then cover and bring to the boil. When the casserole has boiled, remove the lid and lower the heat to a steady simmer for 40–50 minutes, until the beans and meat are tender and the cooking juices have reduced to a soupy sauce. Check for seasoning, and add salt or pepper if need be. Serve very hot in shallow bowls, or with pieces of fried polenta (see page 113).

CREAMED SILVERBEET

BLETTES À LA CRÈME

It was with great delight during our first winter in France that we discovered silverbeet for sale in our local market — only here they call it Swiss chard. Our favourite way of cooking it is in the oven in a gratin dish wiped with butter and garlic, with fresh cream and nutmeg added.

SERVES 6

750 g (1 lb 10 oz) SILVERBEET, WASHED AND TRIMMED
3 OR 4 KNOBS BUTTER
A CLOVE GARLIC, CRUSHED
250 ml (8 fl oz) FRESH CREAM
SALT AND PEPPER

Take a medium-sized gratin dish and rub the surface with butter and crushed garlic.

Preheat the oven to a moderate heat 180°C (350°F; gas mark 4).

Cut the green part of the silverbeet away from the white part. Lightly salt both and steam them very gently for a few minutes. Drain any excess water from the leaves and stalks, and arrange in the gratin dish.

Pour over the fresh cream, grate some nutmeg over the top and cover with a sheet of cooking foil.

Cook in the oven for around 25-40 minutes until the stalks are tender and the cream has thickened slightly.

VEGETARIAN COUSCOUS

COUSCOUS AUX LÉGUMES

Couscous is a North African speciality, but one that France has adopted from its colonial past. There are many versions to be had, most often cooked with lamb and sometimes fish. We have not yet tasted a really outstanding couscous, which is what led me to start making it myself. The secret apparently lies in the proportions of the condiments, with the essential ingredients being chickpeas and, of course, the couscous grain itself. Couscous is not actually a grain, but is made from semolina flour which has been passed through a fine sieve and then dried. It is cooked in a *couscousier*, a traditional pot which divides into two parts, one fitting on top of the other; a bit like a vegetable steamer in principle. The stew cooks in the bottom, while the 'grain' is steamed in the vapours rising from the stew and passing through the tiny sieve-like holes into the top compartment.

This recipe is an adaptation of a Tunisian version of couscous called Mesfouf de Jerba. If you wish to add meat, try it with 800 g (1 lb 12 oz) of lamb shoulder or chicken pieces. The vegetables can be varied depending on the season.

SERVES 6

3 TABLESPOONS OLIVE OIL
2 LARGE ONIONS, PEELED AND SLICED THINLY
3 LEEKS, TRIMMED AND SLICED
2 TABLESPOONS TOMATO PASTE
350 g (12 oz) CANNED OR FRESH TOMATOES, CRUSHED
2 TEASPOONS DRIED RED CHILLI FLAKES OR 1 TEASPOON HOT CHILLI POWDER
1/4 TEASPOON GROUND CORIANDER
1/4 TEASPOON GROUND CARAWAY SEEDS
1/4 TEASPOON GROUND FENNEL SEEDS
1/4 TEASPOON GROUND CUMIN
1/4 TEASPOON GROUND TURMERIC
2–3 CLOVES GARLIC, CRUSHED
SALT AND PEPPER TO TASTE
500 ml (1 pint) WATER
500 g COUSCOUS GRAIN

3–4 CARROTS, PEELED AND SLICED IN JULIENNE STRIPS
4 LARGE POTATOES, PEELED AND CUT INTO CUBES
200 g (7 oz) PEAS
3 COURGETTES, SLICED
450 g (1 lb) CHICKPEAS, SOAKED OVERNIGHT IN COLD
WATER AND PRECOOKED FOR 1 1/2 HOURS, OR CANNED
A HANDFUL FRESHLY CHOPPED PARSLEY TO GARNISH

Heat the olive oil in the bottom of a couscous cooker or a heavy-based cast-iron casserole dish. Add the onions and leeks, and sauté for approximately 5 minutes. (If you wish to include lamb or chicken, add it at the same time and sauté it until the meat releases its juices a little.)

Now add the tomato paste, stirring well, then the crushed tomatoes, red chilli flakes or chilli powder and all the spices, including the garlic. Season with salt, add the water, and simmer for 5 minutes.

In the meantime, rinse the couscous grains in a sieve, and tip them into a large, shallow bowl. Pour in enough boiling salted water to cover the grains by about 1 cm ($^1/_2$ inch). Cover to stop the steam from escaping, and leave for about 10 minutes to allow the couscous grains to absorb the moisture and swell. This is how couscous grain cooks. This step is very important. If the grain has not absorbed enough moisture before you eat it, it will continue to swell in your stomach.

Now add the rest of the vegetables and the chickpeas to the onions and spices. Check that there is enough liquid so that the stew does not dry out, and add a little more water if necessary. Simmer gently until the vegetables are cooked but not mushy.

If you have a *couscousier*, rake the swollen grains with a spoon or fork to remove the lumps, and spoon into the upper compartment. Cover with the lid and let it steam for about 10–15 minutes. If you do not have a *couscousier*, repeat the initial swelling process with the couscous for a second time.

When all the ingredients are cooked, tip the cooked couscous grain into a large serving bowl and add a few knobs of butter or a little olive oil. Spoon over the vegetable stew, which should be quite soupy, and garnish with freshly chopped parsley and Harissa (see page 125).

CARAMELISED TURNIPS
NAVETS CARAMÉLISÉS

Predominantly a winter vegetable, the simple turnip has fallen from favour in recent times. They are extremely versatile though, and have a low calorific value despite their high sugar content. They are particularly good when accompanying fatty meats like lamb, mutton or duck, and are essential in a good hearty vegetable soup. When caramelised, as in the following recipe, their strong flavour softens a little and is particularly appealing. It is advisable to blanch winter turnips for 10 minutes prior to using them, and it is preferable not to peel them in advance as the flesh of the vegetable will discolour.

SERVES 4

500 g (1 lb 2 oz) TURNIPS, PEELED THEN BLANCHED FOR 10
MINUTES
2–3 TABLESPOONS OLIVE OIL OR SEVERAL KNOBS OF
BUTTER
4–6 TABLESPOONS BROWN SUGAR
A HANDFUL OF FRESHLY CHOPPED PARSLEY TO GARNISH
(OPTIONAL)

Cut the turnips into quarters then into eighths.

Heat the oil or butter in a large saucepan on a medium heat and add the turnips. Coat all sides with the oil or butter and sprinkle over half the sugar. Cover the pan and cook steadily, stirring the contents regularly. After about 10 minutes add the rest of the sugar and stir. By now the turnips should be starting to look glazed and slightly golden. Adjust the heat if need be, as you do not want the turnips to burn.

After about 15–20 minutes they should be nicely caramelised and ready to serve. Garnish with freshly chopped parsley, if you wish, and a twist of ground pepper and salt.

BRAISED BRUSSELS SPROUTS

CHOUX DE BRUXELLES POÊLÉS

Definitely a winter vegetable, the first really tender Brussels sprouts start appearing on the market stands a few weeks before Christmas. We are not overly fond of the way the French tend to purée them, but this method of cooking sprouts goes beautifully with the Christmas goose. They are a great accompaniment to game too, especially pheasant. This recipe also works very well with red cabbage, with a few slivers of red pepper thrown in.

SERVES 4

500 g (1 lb 2 oz) NEW SEASON'S BRUSSELS SPROUTS,
TRIMMED AND CLEANED
3 TABLESPOONS OLIVE OIL
50 ml (2 fl oz) RED WINE
BLACK PEPPER AND SEA SALT TO SEASON

In a saucepan, cover the Brussels sprouts with water and bring to the boil. Cook until par-boiled, about 10 minutes. Drain and leave for a few minutes to dry.

Heat the olive oil in a frying pan over a medium heat and add the Brussels sprouts. Brown them gently. Add the red wine and continue cooking steadily until the sprouts are cooked but not mushy. Liberally season with black pepper and sea salt.

BRAISED LEEKS IN RED WINE

POIREAUX AU VIN ROUGE

Around Christmas time, when the weather has turned really cold, the wild vineyard leeks are ready to be gathered. We dress up warmly, climb on our bicycles and head for our friend's vineyard, which has not been treated with any pesticides or herbicides. An hour is enough time to fill a basket with these little vegetables, plenty for our evening meal, and a bagful to snap-freeze for adding to soups and stocks all through winter. You will find cultivated leeks just as delicious prepared this way too.

SERVES 4

4–6 MEDIUM-SIZED LEEKS
2 TABLESPOONS OLIVE OIL
125 ml (4 fl oz) RED WINE
2 TABLESPOONS GOOD STOCK OR 1 STOCK CUBE
(BEEF, CHICKEN OR VEGETABLE BOUILLON)

Having trimmed the bottoms and tops of the leeks (leave some of the green part of the leek), slice them into quarters lengthways, until you get to just below the white part of the leek. Fill the sink with cold water and wash the leeks several times to get rid of the grit and dirt. Shake off any excess water or pat dry.

In a heavy-bottomed frying pan, heat the olive oil and add the leeks, and sauté for several minutes before covering with a lid for a further 3–4 minutes. Add the wine and the stock and cover again, reducing the heat. Let the leeks braise for about 10 minutes, or until they are tender. This will depend on the size of the leeks you use. Remove the leeks from the pan with a slotted spoon, arrange on a serving plate and keep warm.

Raise the heat in the pan again and reduce the wine and cooking juices until you have about 60 ml (2 fl oz). Pour over the leeks and serve.

POLENTA WITH PARMESAN

POLENTA AU PARMESAN

A traditional dish of northern Italy, this cornmeal porridge is a delicious alternative to potatoes, and goes particularly well with braised meats and game. It is also delicious the next day, brushed with olive oil and grilled until crisp on the outside, and served with a bean casserole.

SERVES 6

1 LITRE (2 PINTS) WATER, SALTED
250 g (9 oz) CORNMEAL
60–70 g (2–3 oz) UNSALTED BUTTER
75 g (3 oz) PARMESAN, FRESHLY GRATED

Boil the water in a large saucepan. While the water is boiling slowly sprinkle in the cornmeal grains, stirring all the time until all the grain is mixed in the water. Cook for 20 minutes, stirring continuously with a wooden spoon, almost as you would porridge. The mixture will start to come away from the sides of the pot and form a ball. Now add the butter and the parmesan cheese. Mix well and turn out into a warmed serving dish. Serve hot.

If conserving until the next day, turn out onto a damp plate, spreading the polenta into a thick layer. Leave to cool then cut into squares or diamond shapes. The following day, coat the outside with olive oil and grill.

POTATOES IN CREAM

POMMES DE TERRE À LA DAUPHINOISE

In France, as in all of Europe, the tasty varieties and ways of cooking this simple vegetable are many. This recipe is particularly good in winter with red meats, and equally in summer with grilled or barbecued meats. Although the cream may seem heavy, this style of cooking potatoes adds moisture and texture to a meal. If cream is not your thing, try substituting a good meat stock instead.

SERVES 4–6

1 kg (2 lb 3 oz) FLOURY POTATOES, PEELED AND SLICED
INTO ROUNDS
1 LARGE CLOVE GARLIC
3–4 KNOBS BUTTER
FRESHLY GROUND SEA SALT AND PEPPER, TO TASTE
FRESHLY GROUND NUTMEG
1 LARGE ONION, COARSELY SLICED (OPTIONAL)
250 ml (8 fl oz) CREAM
SEVERAL SPRIGS FRESH THYME

Rub the surface of a reasonably large gratin dish with the garlic, leaving the pieces of garlic in the bottom of the dish.

Add 2–3 knobs of butter, then layer the dish with the potato slices, seasoning each layer with salt and pepper, nutmeg and the sliced onion, if you are using it.

When the dish is full, pour over the cream and place another knob or two of butter on top. Sprinkle generously with fresh thyme and cover the dish with some foil. Place in a medium oven, 180°C (350°F; gas mark 4), for 60–90 minutes, until cooked, removing the foil for the last 20 minutes so that the top browns nicely.

PEARS IN RED WINE

POIRES AU VIN ROUGE

This is a sumptuous winter dessert best served at the end of a well-balanced menu, as the pears and syrup are rich and tangy. It is preferable to use a light, dry red wine — claret style is ideal. Do not use any cheap old plonk as the sauce will not benefit from your economies. The pears should be firm and ripe, like a Bartlett, Bosc, William or Louise Bonne. When purchasing the pears, make sure they have a flattish bottom so they will stand up on the serving dish.

SERVES 4

4 FIRM, RIPE PEARS
1/2 LEMON
750 ml (1 1/2 pints) DRY, CLARET-STYLE RED WINE
150 g (5 oz) SUGAR
1 STRIP LEMON PEEL, 5 cm (2 inches)
1 CINNAMON STICK, CRACKED
4 WHOLE PEPPERCORNS
4 WHOLE CLOVES
1 VANILLA BEAN, SLIT LENGTHWAYS

Peel the pears and core them from the base, taking care not to damage the stalk at the top. Rub each pear with lemon as you go to avoid any discoloration of the flesh.

In a good-sized saucepan, combine the wine, sugar, lemon peel and spices, and bring the liquid to the boil. Reduce the heat and simmer, stirring occasionally, for about 5 minutes. Add the pears and place a saucer, upside-down, on top of the pears so they remain covered by the liquid. Cook the pears for about 20–25 minutes at a bare simmer, turning from time to time, until they are just tender. Turn the heat off and let the pears cool.

Transfer the pears to a separate dish and put to one side. Put the saucepan back onto a medium-high heat, reducing the liquid to about 250 ml (8 fl oz). This will take about 20–30 minutes. It will now be quite thick and syrupy in consistency. Strain and allow to cool.

Place the pears, sitting up, on individual plates and spoon over the syrup. Serve at room temperature with a dash of crème fraîche to one side.

APPLE UPSIDE-DOWN TART

TARTE TATIN

According to culinary legend, Tarte Tatin was discovered by chance when an apple tart was dropped inadvertently upside-down on the top of a cooking stove, thereby caramelising the fruit. Then the Tatin sisters made it famous in their popular turn-of-the-century restaurant. Now you will find it on the menu at Les Mimosas.

When you tire of using apples try fresh pears, and at the height of the summer it is superb with nectarines. For a lighter touch, replace the pâte brisée (shortcrust pastry) with puff pastry.

SERVES 4–6

6–8 APPLES DEPENDING ON SIZE, PEELED, CORED, QUARTERED
120 g (3 oz) CASTOR SUGAR
A FEW KNOBS BUTTER, THE SIZE OF YOUR THUMBNAIL, ABOUT 80 g (3 oz) IN ALL
250 g (9 oz) PÂTE BRISÉE (SEE PAGE 121) OR PUFF PASTRY

Take a deepish 24-cm (10-inch) flan dish, sprinkle 60 g (2 oz) castor sugar evenly over the bottom, and lay 2 or 3 small knobs of butter evenly around the base.

Starting from the middle, place the peeled, cored and quartered pieces of apple, peeled side down, on top of the sugar and butter knobs. Arrange as neatly and symmetrically as you can. Sprinkle another 60 g (2 oz) of castor sugar over the apples and place a few more knobs of butter intermittently over the apples.

Roll out the pastry to a size slightly larger than the flan dish. Place the pastry over the fruit and sugar and tuck loosely inside the edge of the dish, so that the fruit is contained within the lid of pastry. Place the dish in a hot oven, 230°C (450°F; gas mark 8), as near to the bottom as possible, for about 25–30 minutes or until the fruit and sugar is caramelised and almost burning. If you use a transparent dish, you will be able to see when the caramelisation has reached just the right stage.

When the tart is cooked, remove it from the oven, loosen the edges with a metal spatula and immediately turn it out on to a serving dish by putting the serving dish, upside-down, over the tart and inverting them together.

Serve warm with fresh cream.

APPLE CRUMBLE

POMMES À LA PEAU DE CRAPAUD

There seems to be nothing quite like apple crumble in French cuisine. In fact, when we served it to our French friends, André said that it resembled *la peau d'un crapaud* — the skin of a toad — which is reasonably accurate. However, it did not stop him from demolishing a couple of platefuls. After all, fresh from the oven, with fresh cream drizzled over, it is pretty irresistible. Apricots, rhubarb and peaches make good substitutes for the apples.

SERVES 4

225 g (8 oz) PLAIN FLOUR (OR MIXED 50/50 WITH ROLLED OATS)
180 g (6 oz) RAW SUGAR
125 g (4 oz) BUTTER
2–3 LARGE COOKING APPLES
PINCH OF CINNAMON POWDER

To make the crumble, measure the flour and sugar into a bowl. Grate the butter into the bowl and rub it into the flour and sugar until it resembles the texture of breadcrumbs.

Peel the apples and slice them, not too finely, layering the slices in an ovenproof dish. Add 125 ml (4 fl oz) water and sprinkle over the cinnamon powder.

Sprinkle over the crumble mixture to get a good layer 1–2 cm ($^1/_2$–1 inch) thick, then add a little raw sugar and a knob or two of butter.

Bake in an oven at 200°C (400°F; gas mark 6) until bubbling, about 30–40 minutes.

RICH CHOCOLATE CUSTARD CREAM

CRÈME AU CHOCOLAT

Crème au chocolat must remain one of the most popular desserts of all time. As chocolate lovers, we have eaten our fair share. They have often been good, sometimes indifferent, and if we have been lucky, exceptional. The recipe that follows falls into the third category, and is made in the traditional French way as a baked custard. It is not difficult, needing only simple preparation and 25 minutes of cooking.

We serve these at Les Mimosas in small white ramekins or old ovenproof demi-tasse coffee cups, with a curl or two of chocolate or orange zest on top. Use high quality, dark chocolate with 70% cocoa.

SERVES 6–8

500 ml (1 pint) CREAM
200 g (7 oz) DARK, BITTER CHOCOLATE, BROKEN IN PIECES
100 g (3 oz) SUGAR
4 EGG YOLKS
1 TEASPOON VANILLA EXTRACT
CHOCOLATE AND/OR ORANGE ZEST FOR GARNISH

Preheat the oven to 180°C (350°F; gas mark 4).

In a heavy saucepan, combine the cream and the broken pieces of chocolate, melting them over a gentle heat, stirring all the while until the mixture is smooth, about 5 minutes. Whisk in the sugar, then the egg yolks, one at a time, then the vanilla extract.

Strain the mixture into 6–8 small ramekins and place in a deep baking pan. Add enough hot water to the pan to reach halfway up the sides of the ramekins. Bake for approximately 25 minutes, or until the tops have just set. Remove the ramekins from the baking pan and set aside to cool.

Just before serving, run a vegetable peeler or zester along the side of a bar of chocolate and/or an orange, allowing the curls to fall on top of the mousse.

EXTRA SPECIAL CHOCOLATE CAKE

FONDANT AU CHOCOLAT

This should really be called 'Devil's cake' because it is so rich that no self-respecting healthy person should ever attempt to eat it — but they do! Made with almond meal, bitter dark chocolate with 70% cocoa, and 6 eggs, it remains moist and dense after cooking, and makes a superb dessert served on its own or with a dab of crème fraîche or a fruit coulis to cut the richness.

FOR THE CAKE

185 g (7 oz) BITTER DARK CHOCOLATE
185 g (7 oz) UNSALTED BUTTER
165 g (6 oz) BROWN SUGAR
6 EGGS, SEPARATED
185 g (7 oz) ALMOND MEAL
PINCH OF SALT

FOR THE ICING

125 ml (4 fl oz) CREAM
250 g (9 oz) BITTER DARK CHOCOLATE
TOASTED ALMOND FLAKES OR FRESH BERRY FRUITS TO DECORATE

Line a 25-cm (10-inch) springform cake tin with foil. Butter the foil then lightly dust with flour. Put to one side.

Melt the chocolate in a bain-marie, or in the microwave, then cool slightly. Cream the unsalted butter and add the sugar, beating until the mixture is light and fluffy. Add the egg yolks, one by one, mixing each one thoroughly into the mixture. Next beat in the cooled chocolate, and gradually add the almond meal.

In a copper bowl, beat the egg whites and salt until they form soft peaks. Fold a large spoonful of egg white into the cake mixture, then add a third of the egg whites, folding gently, and finally the rest of the egg whites. Incorporate thoroughly.

Spoon the mixture into the prepared baking tin and bake for 20 minutes at 190°C (375°F; gas mark 5), then drop the temperature to 180°C (350°F; gas mark 4) for another 40–45 minutes. When cooked, the cake should be soft and moist when the centre is touched with the tip of your finger.

Place the cake, still in its tin, on a damp tea towel and allow to cool. When it is completely cool, remove from the tin and carefully peel away the foil.

TO ICE THE CAKE

Scald the cream and add the chocolate. Stir the mixture with a wire whisk until the chocolate has completely melted and the mixture is smooth.

Stand the saucepan in cold water to help the icing to cool. When it has reached room temperature pour it over the top of the cake, and spread evenly with a spatula. Sprinkle with toasted almonds or fresh berry fruits, to garnish.

GENERAL

SALAD DRESSING
VINAIGRETTE

No cook should be without a favourite basic vinaigrette recipe. In France, where salad is consumed in great quantities, the style of dressing varies widely. In summer, we eat plate after plate of juicy, sun-ripened tomatoes topped with a creamy mustard vinaigrette and fresh herbs; in winter, a selection of sharp-tasting salad greens, like frisée, complemented by a warm walnut dressing topped with lardons (bacon pieces) or *gésiers* (preserved duck gizzards). In springtime, artichokes and asparagus are drizzled with generous amounts of garlic and balsamic-vinegar dressing.

Everyone has their own way of making a dressing. For some, a small airtight jar is the most practical for mixing ingredients. Here, the dressing is made in the bottom of a salad bowl first then the salad greens are added and tossed. Some cooks crush a clove of garlic under the blade of a knife before rubbing the empty bowl with the aromatic clove. This is especially effective for a plain green salad with a simple dressing of oil and vinegar. In Provence, the garlic can often be found in hearty, hot chunks hiding unexpectedly between the salad leaves.

One thing is certain, the salad leaves must always be well washed in cold water (at least twice) to remove grit and dirt, and then dried thoroughly in order that the dressing may be carried by the salad leaves. Whatever the recipe, a vinaigrette is a very personal thing and the search for the ideal flavour seems to be a lifelong one.

BASIC VINAIGRETTE

1 PART VINEGAR (MALT, TARRAGON, BALSAMIC, SHERRY, WHITE WINE, RED WINE, SHALLOT, THYME, WALNUT, RASPBERRY, GARLIC . . .)
2 PARTS OIL (OLIVE, SUNFLOWER, WALNUT, HAZELNUT, GRAPE-SEED, HERB, SESAME, RAPE-SEED, SOYA . . .)
FRESHLY GROUND BLACK PEPPER AND SEA SALT
2 PINCHES SUGAR
1 CLOVE GARLIC, CRUSHED (OPTIONAL)

Pour the vinegar into a glass jar or salad bowl, and add the sugar and salt (These will not dissolve in oil).

Add the oil, pepper and garlic and mix thoroughly with a fork. Leave to stand for at least half an hour.

NOTE: To make a cream dressing, halve the quantity of oil and add some liquid cream, beating rapidly with a fork, just before the salad greens are added to the dressing. To make a herb dressing, add a handful of your favourite chopped herbs to the basic vinaigrette recipe.

MUSTARD VINAIGRETTE

1 TABLESPOON DIJON MUSTARD
1 TABLESPOON RED-WINE OR TARRAGON VINEGAR
PEPPER AND SALT, TO TASTE
3 TABLESPOONS SUNFLOWER OIL

Mix the mustard, vinegar and salt in a small bowl.

Add the sunflower oil slowly, stirring steadily, rather as you would when making a mayonnaise, until the dressing has a smooth, even consistency. Adjust the seasoning to your liking, and pour it over a plate of freshly sliced, sun-ripened tomatoes. Garnish with freshly ground pepper and the herb of your choice.

MAYONNAISE

MAYONNAISE CLASSIQUE

Making mayonnaise can sometimes be tricky until you are familiar with the process. Once you have mastered a few basic rules, a fresh mayo can be whipped up in no time to the benefit of everyone's tastebuds. Add anything to the sauce once it is made — freshly chopped herbs, roasted vegetables, ground garlic or coriander, fish or shellfish, saffron or chillis. The basic rules are: make sure all your ingredients are at room temperature before you start; do not add the ingredients too quickly or the sauce will curdle; do not over-beat the mayonnaise.

2 EGG YOLKS
PEPPER AND SALT
DASH OF TARRAGON VINEGAR
2 TEASPOONS DIJON MUSTARD
375–500 ml (12–16 fl oz) OLIVE OIL (AS A RULE, 1 LARGE
EGG YOLK WILL CONSUME 250 ml (8 fl oz) OLIVE OIL)

Place the egg yolks, pepper, salt and tarragon vinegar in a medium-sized bowl. Stir briskly with a wooden spoon or metal whisk. Add the Dijon mustard.

As soon as the mixture is smooth begin adding the oil, drizzling it in almost drop by drop, while continuing to stir at the same time, in the same direction. Do not beat the mayonnaise too hard — the whiteness of the sauce will depend on the consistency and rapidity of stirring.

When the sauce begins to increase in volume the oil can be added more quickly, in a gentle trickle, until all the oil is combined.

Check seasoning, turn out into an airtight glass jar, and store in a cool place.

NOTE: If the mayonnaise begins to separate, add a dash of boiling water or lemon juice. The lemon juice will make the sauce whiter.

A GOOD SHORT PASTRY

PÂTE BRISÉE

225 g (8 oz) SIFTED PLAIN FLOUR
1 TEASPOON BAKING POWDER
PINCH OF SALT
125 g (4 oz) CHILLED UNSALTED BUTTER
1 EGG YOLK, BEATEN (OPTIONAL)
ICED WATER TO MIX (ABOUT 3 TABLESPOONS)

Mix the flour, baking powder and salt in a large bowl, and rub in the chilled butter with your fingertips until the mixture resembles breadcrumbs.

Stir in the beaten egg yolk, then the cold water, and mix to a very stiff dough. Do not overwork the pastry as it will become tough. Wrap it in some cling film and chill in the refrigerator for half an hour.

When ready to use, roll out quickly, handling as little as possible, to the size and thickness you require. Bake in a hot oven, 200°C (400°F; gas mark 6) for about 10–15 minutes or until golden.

This makes about 400 g (14 oz) of pastry.

RICH SWEETENED SHORTCRUST PASTRY

PÂTE SABLÉE

1 EGG
125 g (4 oz) VERY FINE CASTOR SUGAR
250 g (9 oz) SIFTED PLAIN FLOUR
125 g (4 oz) CHILLED UNSALTED BUTTER
ICING SUGAR TO MIX

In a large bowl, beat the egg and sugar together thoroughly. Rub in the flour and knead in the butter.

Quickly work the pastry into a ball using icing sugar instead of flour to stop it sticking. Wrap in cling film and rest in the refrigerator for at least an hour.

Roll out with icing sugar when ready and bake in a hot oven, 200°C (400°F; gas mark 6), for about 10–15 minutes, or until golden brown.

This makes about 500 g (1 lb 2 oz) of pastry.

RYE BREAD

PAIN DE SEIGLE

The French are passionate about good bread, and they love to discuss the pros and cons of what and who makes the best bread and why. With the advent of modern factory-prepared breads the true artisans or craft breadmakers have demanded a special appellation for their highly skilled practice of breadmaking, and rightly so. In our opinion the famous Parisian baker Poilâne makes the best rye bread on earth! Our house rye bread is not a patch on his bread but it is very good and takes little effort to make. For a lighter version, try a lighter flour like 5-cereals or mix the two 50/50.

FOR THE STARTER

100 ml (3 fl oz) WARM WATER
1 PACKET OR 8 g (1/4 oz) DRIED YEAST
1–2 TEASPOONS HONEY OR BLACK STRAP MOLASSES

Mix all these in a glass bowl, cover with a linen tea towel and place in a warm draught-free place for 5–15 minutes.

FOR THE REST

200 g (7 oz) WHITE FLOUR
500 g (1 lb 2 oz) RYE FLOUR
A GOOD TEASPOON FINE SALT
350 ml (12 fl oz) WARM WATER

Measure out the flour, add the salt and mix well. Make a well in the centre and when the starter is 'working' and foaming nicely, pour it into the well and mix with a knife. Add the rest of the warm water, discard the knife and start working the dough with your hands until the flour and liquid are combined. Knead with the heel of your hand for a maximum of 5 minutes on a flat, floured surface. Make a ball with the dough and place it on a metal baking tray or in an earthenware bread-pot that has been oiled. Rub some olive oil into the dome of the ball, and cut 4 diagonal lines in the top, 2

one way and 2 the other way, over the top of the first two. Dust the top with rye flour and cover with a linen tea towel. Place in a warm, draught-free space — a hot water cupboard is ideal — for about an hour, until the loaf has doubled in size. In the meantime, heat the oven to 245°C (475°F; gas mark 9). It should be very hot. If you have a fan-assisted oven, turn the fan off if you can, as it will dry out the dough.

Place the loaf in the oven and cook for about 20–25 minutes, until golden brown and crisp.

To test that your bread is cooked, tap the base with your finger; if it sounds hollow it is done. Remove from the oven and lay the bread on its side in such a way that the air can get to the bottom, or on a cake rack — that way the bottom crust of the bread will remain crisp also.

A good rye bread will keep well for 4–5 days, if it lasts that long.

CHILLI PEPPER PASTE

HARISSA

We discovered this amazing North African condiment one day while browsing in the Friday produce market in Béziers. At this particular stall, the paste was home-made and available for sale by weight. Denis, being a chilli addict, immediately bought 250 g of the stuff, which was then wrapped up carefully in 3 sealed plastic bags. He nurtured his purchase all morning and it was not until we got into the car to come home that the significance of the 3 plastic bags became apparent. The car filled up with the most amazing garlic pong we had ever had the misfortune to encounter. Windows were rapidly wound down, and once home the package was promptly placed in an airtight jar and popped dubiously into the refrigerator. Despite the unfortunate odour, it was a taste sensation, and to this day we have never found a brew quite as good.

Harissa is readily available in tubes and cans here in France, but they never match up to our original experience, so now we make our own. Use it sparingly (if you do not like too much heat) with pasta, soups, couscous, casseroles or to accompany spicy meat or vegetable dishes.

60 g (2 oz) FRESH, RED CHILLIS, SEEDED
2 LARGE CLOVES GARLIC
1/4 TEASPOON SEA SALT
75 ml (3 fl oz) EXTRA VIRGIN OLIVE OIL

Soak the chillis in warm water for 1 hour. Drain and place in a blender or food processor with the garlic and salt. Process to a fine paste, adding the olive oil as you go.

Store in an airtight jar in the refrigerator for 1–2 weeks, covered with a small amount of olive oil.

CUSTARD CREAM

CRÈME ANGLAISE

A great cold custard cream for garnishing rich chocolate cakes, fruit tarts and charlottes, or mixing with a fruit coulis — its uses are many. It is best made in advance, keeps well for 2–3 days in an airtight container in the refrigerator, and is easy to flavour with liqueurs, pralines and caramel. The delicate procedure of combining the egg yolks with the hot milk is the most crucial as the yolks can curdle if they are heated too quickly.

MAKES APPROXIMATELY 500 ml

625 ml (20 fl oz) MILK
1 VANILLA BEAN, SPLIT WITH A SHARP KNIFE
6 EGG YOLKS
100 g (3 oz) CASTOR SUGAR

Bring the milk to the boil with the vanilla bean. Beat the egg yolks and sugar with a whisk until they are pale and creamy. Remove the vanilla beans. Carefully pour the boiling milk into the egg mixture and whisk.

Return the mixture to the saucepan and stir patiently over a very low heat, until the custard coats the back of a wooden spoon. Strain the custard through a very fine sieve and allow to cool. Store in the refrigerator in a sealed container.

INDEX